THE AMAZING ADVENTURES OF A
MARGINALLY
SUCCESSFUL MUSICIAN

Bill Cinque

iUniverse, Inc.
New York   Bloomington

THE AMAZING ADVENTURES OF A MARGINALLY SUCCESSFUL MUSICIAN

iUniverse books may be ordered through booksellers or by contacting:

iUniverse
1663 Liberty Drive
Bloomington, IN 47403
www.iuniverse.com
1-800-Authors (1-800-288-4677)

ISBN: 978-1-4401-1567-7 (pbk)
ISBN: 978-1-4401-1569-1 (cloth)
ISBN: 978-1-4401-1568-4 (ebk)

Printed in the United States of America

iUniverse rev. date: 1/4/2010

Contents

INTRODUCTION

This is my first book. It's taken longer than expected. I recently learned that Charles Darwin didn't publish the Origin of Species until he was 50, so I guess I'm right on schedule. I don't know the difference between a foreword and an introduction, so I'll just start here. It's been said that you should write what you know. For me, fame and fortune were topics to be immediately eliminated. "Write about your life experience," was my high school English teacher's advice. That left me with only 2 choices. I figured no one was interested in a book called "WHY JENNIFER ANISTON WON'T RETURN MY CALLS", so here's a book about my life as a musician. I have considered writing this book many times in the last 10 years. This is the first time it ever got out of my head and onto the page. My sincere hope is that it sheds a little light on some real world musical situations.

The next bit of advice I got was to make sure the title of the book was short and catchy. It has to be memorable or no one will buy it. I beg to differ. After all, you bought this one and I'll bet you can't recite the title without looking at the cover. Am I right?

This book contains some facts, many opinions, several amusing anecdotes and a handful of arcane references, all aimed at aiding the working musician. It is part "HOW TO" and part history book. I feel it is equally important to declare that this does not contain the secret formula for becoming wealthy and famous. This book is not titled "HOW TO GET A RECORD DEAL". This is simply a collection of my observations and experiences in 30 years of playing music for a living. Maybe it can help you make a living in music.

Many musicians feel that the elusive major label record deal is the only true measure of success. Maybe some of them will reconsider after reading this. Hopefully, you'll find this an easy read. I have done my level best to inform and entertain, using stories, charts, graphs and dream sequences to help illustrate certain situations. I was bold enough to throw in a few ridiculous cartoons drawn by me, requiring the following disclaimer:

These stick figure pencil drawings are fictional and are not meant to depict any other stick figure pencil drawings, living or dead. They are, however, created by a professional stick figure pencil drawer, namely, me. Attention amateur SFPDs, do not try this at home. Side effects can be lead poisoning, eye poke, graphite induced malaria and erasurephobia, all of which are clearly outlined in my next book, "THE # 2 PENCIL: TOOL OR WEAPON?"

Please consult your physician, cartoonist and/or graphic artist before attempting such drawings. Remember, pocket protectors save lives.

I've performed with many platinum selling acts and many more acts that couldn't get arrested. Come to think of it, a few managed to get arrested anyway. I've been the front man, the sideman and the last minute sub. I've played state fairs and state prisons, arenas and pubs. (I swear to God that rhyme was unintentional.) All of this has made for a great life and hopefully a great read.

This book is full of mood swings. I often fell into some dark humor. This was not just a way to get a laugh. In many cases, I was revealing some of my deepest feelings about the music, musicians and business I have come to know, love and hate. Sometimes, I approached a serious topic with some comic relief. Other times, I couldn't help but be angered by the silliness and lunacy that surrounds the simplest club gig. In essence, 30 years of playing music has tilted my world slightly. I see the comedy in the drama and vice versa. I have made no attempt to correct my vision in this book. I wrote what I wrote when I wrote it based on my observations and feelings. I even used a few dirty words. If you are easily offended, I suggest skipping over the chapters titled MUSICIAN'S HOROSCOPE and IMAGINARY LETTERS. I stand by my writing and take whatever accolades and criticisms that may arise. I hope you can hang in there with me to the last page.

Speaking of accolades and criticisms, how do authors get those great reviews printed on the jacket of the book? You know, the blurbs that say stuff like, "This book is an American classic." "The best thriller in decades. I couldn't put it down." How did someone read the book before it was printed? These reviewer dudes would have to have read the book at least 2 weeks earlier because the printing process takes at least that long. I know for a fact that it usually takes about 2 weeks to read a book. This means the reviewer dude had to have had the book a month before it came out. That's physically impossible! (Unless he's using time travel and I have it on good authority that the Incredible Way Back Machine won't be perfected for another 86 years.) This all brings me to the logical conclusion that these book jacket critiques are a total scam. Aha! You've been found out, my wordsmith brethren!

Still, now that I have thrown my hat into the literary arena, I must fight fire with fire and keep up with the proverbial Jones'. You know what they say. Either you hunt in the tall grass with the big dogs or you sit on the front porch. Or something. Was it the front porch? Maybe it was a gazebo or a lanai but I'm positive about the canine reference. Anyway, I have to play the game, so here are my reviews. I will be the first author in history to openly declare that they are totally falsified.

"This book is right on the money! Insightful and colorful, an incredibly accurate description of the world of music"--Bob, the crazy guy who yells at traffic.

"Man, I would love to have lived long enough to read this book. I understand it's quite entertaining. Sadly, I was killed in 1876. Man, timing is everything." -George Armstrong Custer

"I read this book in between wives. It's my type of humor."-Bluebeard

Actually, I do have a few real ones. These are all from my great friend, Michael Lloyd. Michael has been a world class producer for decades. He produced the sound track for DIRTY DANCING. He has sold millions of records and worked with artists such as Frank Sinatra, Belinda Carlisle, Erica Nicole, Barry Manilow.

And me.

I'll let you insert your own punch line here. I've already given you several full pages of "clever". Frankly, I'm exhausted. Anyway, Michael was kind enough to give me a few quotes. Here are the unadulterated words of one of pop music's greatest icons.

"This book is certainly worth reading...hopefully by someone else."

"This book is terrific. It fits perfectly under the TV to keep it level."

I thought that would be the end of it. No such luck. He had more to say.

"I've read a lot of books. Maybe I don't need to read this one."

Apparently, Michael softened up a bit and retreated to the standard fare, playing the "niceties" card.

"Great reading. Great fun. Great book."

"I love it. It's filled with stories and ideas that are really great."

"I highly recommend this to anyone that loves music and musicians."

Well played, my friend. Well played, indeed.

I guess I'll have some more real reviews soon enough, maybe even from you. Take your best shot. I promise I won't let the good reviews go to my head. I'll probably ignore the bad ones, but feel free to send them along anyway. Send all correspondence to billcinque.com.

Enough of this prelude nonsense. Let's get to it. Let's examine the area of music that is very often overlooked. Together, we will explore the world located somewhere between unemployment and rock stardom. Welcome to the world of the blue collar, working class musician.
Meet you at the last page!!

THANK YOU

I always wondered if authors ever really wanted to thank people for their support. Were they truly appreciative or were they just saying so in print out of obligation? I mean, there could be some pretty severe backlash from saying, "Thanks to my next door neighbor, Timmy for all his support. I wish my bitch of a wife would have had a little faith in me." Luckily, I have had incredible support from friends and family my entire life. That's probably why I've been able to stay in the game so long. The following thanks are well deserved.

I would love to say thanks to my entire family. To my brother, Steve, my best friend and the first musician I ever met. To my sisters, Mary and Pat who managed to applaud while holding rosary beads, praying that my '78 Chevy Chevette would make it home. To my sister, Teri, who showed us all that it's never too late to catch a dream, and to my little brother, David, who possesses the greatest rock 'n' roll spirit of all time. To Marion and Vincent, who changed my life with the stroke of a pen. To Angel, my almost-kinda-pretty close to step daughter who always makes life a little easier for a lot of us. To Riley, whose gift of my good luck guitar strap has been with me on every gig for the past 10 years and will hopefully be with me for the next 10 years. To Trisha, the strongest woman in the world and in my eyes, the only woman in the world.

To Mom and Dad, who endured my Led Zeppelin records being played way too loud for way too long and still showed up at table #1 in a little place called Peppercorn's to listen to me do the only thing I ever wanted to do.

CHAPTER ONE: WHOA!!

I do mean Whoa!! I realize this is chapter one. You would think it should be called GETTING STARTED. Not a chance. Here's why.

Everyone has a preconceived picture of a musician. It is sometimes the image of the bigger than life rock star in a stretch limo. Other times, it's that of the unemployed slacker living on a friend's couch. It's either world tours and stadiums or your kid brother playing Wipe Out in your parent's garage. When a girl tells her dad she's dating a musician, Dad grabs the shotgun. All of you have ideas of how a musician walks, talks and acts, so you're not really starting at the beginning at all.

Rock stars are rare birds, indeed. You almost never get to meet one. Mostly, they are admired from afar. Their fans flock to their concerts, listen to their songs on the radio and download the latest tunes the moment they are released.

Every musician's dream is to have that kind of success. The chances of being a rock star are slim. Actually, you have a better chance of being hit by lightning while holding a winning lottery ticket. By all means, give stardom your best shot. Meanwhile, some elements of this book may help you on your way up or on the way…elsewhere.

At the other end of the musical spectrum, there is the garage band. These are the kids with all the enthusiasm in the world, trying to make as much music as possible before the neighbors call the police. The garage band often has more drive than talent. The garage band is usually made up of younger, less experienced musicians who have yet to be jaded by the hardships of the business. They are naïve and fearless. They are convinced that they are the next big thing. God bless the garage band.

Everybody's trying to be a rock star. At the same time, the streets are lined with unemployed musicians. Is there anything in between? Of course there is. That would be the old fashioned, blue collar, working musician. Bet you never thought of that!

You think you understand the world of music because you watch MTV and VH1. You read Rolling Stone cover to cover. You've become addicted to Behind the Music. You practice your instrument everyday. Many people tell you you're very talented, yet you can't seem to make it in music. You have a thousand questions. Again, I say "whoa." Slow down. I'll try to get you some answers.

Playing music isn't like most other occupations. In most career paths, you are promoted based on years of service, hard work and positive results. It's the classic American Dream. You start in the mail room, work your way up to middle management and 20 years later, become Vice President. (You'll never become president. That bastard is the owner's only son and he's 15 years younger than you.) You pay your dues and work overtime. You impress the boss and take on more responsibility. You rise up the corporate ladder.

This rarely happens as a musician. Huge success can befall a 15 year old who doesn't write the songs he performs and can barely sing. At the same moment said 15 year old is on the radio making money hand over prepubescent fist, there is a brilliant singer/songwriter serving fries on Sunset Blvd. This is no joke.

It can be a heartbreaking business for most. Many a musician has invested blood, sweat and tears to perfect his craft, pay his dues and hone his skills. Often, he will watch helplessly as the less talented pass him on the road to success. Certainly, success should not be measured in just dollars, but let's be realistic. You do want to be recognized for your talent and you do want to be compensated. That very often translates into dollars. Gigs, ticket sales, radio play, TV placements, CD and t-shirts sales all play a role in your success. It doesn't necessarily mean millions, but it is your living. It can be tough.

BOTTOM LINE:

A separate book could be written on why "JOHNNY GOT A RECORD DEAL and BOBBY DIDN'T". There are too many factors. The times, the economy, the record company, the political climate and even the artist's sense of fashion can all play a part in why an executive might take a chance on you. That is why this book is not titled "HOW TO GET A RECORD DEAL". I never got a record deal, so I'm not going to give advice about that. I will, however, tell you to sit up straight. Stop slouching!

Some of these same factors apply to getting a gig at the corner pub. Why did the other band get the gig? Who knows? Well, actually, I do. Thank goodness you bought/borrowed/ stole this book. You can learn a little something about being a professional musician. You might not get the chance to play Carnegie Hall (although I did), but you could take a step up from the happy hour at the Secret Asian Man Café, where your band is advertised prominently on a paper plate tacked to the front door. The 8 foot, tri-color, neon marquee is reserved to announce today's dinner special: Yummy Slow Puppy.

Remember to tip your bartender.

MY FIRST GIG

My first gig was in a whorehouse.

No kidding. I didn't know it at the time, but I was told the next day that it was a brothel. This was way back in 1976. I was a senior in high school. I was in a garage band with a few friends. One day, the singer told us that we had a gig at a little bar in Yonkers, NY. We were all high school students who were not old enough to play in clubs. We were told it was perfectly legal, as alcohol was not sold in this particular establishment. Exactly what was being sold in that establishment was never mentioned.

I walked 1.44 miles (thank you, Mapquest) with my Les Paul copy with no case to the club. The rest of the band was just loading in when I arrived. It's a good thing the station wagon was parked right in front, as this club had no name, no sign and no visible address. We walked into the dimly lit room. The windows were covered with drapes. The doorway to the restrooms had one of those beaded curtains. It was all very hippie looking. Incense was burning. A guy wearing bracelets, necklaces, multiple earrings, a vest and no shirt stood behind the bar. He explained that they had yet to get a liquor license but I only wanted a Pepsi. He told me they had none, but they had these flavored drinks made of what seemed to be some kind of syrup and seltzer, like home made soda pop. I had one and it was tasty.

The band set up in time to play for our 3 friends who showed up. A few guys walked in the front door and passed the stage. I assumed they were going to the bathroom. There was one beautiful blond girl who came out of the back and smiled. She was wearing a headband and a buckskin fringed top, as if she were a Native American extra in a John Wayne movie. A little while later, the 2 guys and the girl came out front to listen for a moment. I think she tipped the band a few dollars and then they left. The room was empty.

The band didn't know many songs. We played a few Santana tunes and then a few Hendrix tunes. We jammed a lot. It was all very cool for us. I was happy to be doing a gig of any kind. It was a bit surreal, with the lighting, the vibe and the total lack of an audience. I guess we stopped around midnight. We said thank you and goodnight to the bartender guy and I proceeded to walk home through the rather sketchy neighborhood of South Yonkers with my caseless guitar over my shoulder.

At 10 o'clock the next morning. I was on the bus with the Yonkers High lacrosse team. On the way to the game, I mentioned to a few of my team mates that I had just played my first gig ten hours earlier. As I talked, a few of the guys became curious. "The place on the west side of Riverdale Ave.? Are you kidding me? That's a whore house." "No!" I said. "Whores and drugs. I know the place. It's a damn whore house," my teammate insisted. Another spoke up. "You mean, WAS a whore house. It burned down early this morning. I live right down the street. I saw the fire engines." Later that week, I saw the burned out building for myself. Years later, I worked for City Hall. My office mate, Celia, knew everything about the city. She was a lifelong resident of Yonkers and was always happy to share a story. I asked her a few questions about that no name club. "Oh, the place where all the hookers used to hang out? Yeah, the cops used to bust the place every few months, but there was never any real trouble."

BOTTOM LINE:

Looking back, my first gig was for no money, with no audience and a touch of arson. I think that's the Trifecta for gigs. As for the drugs, I never saw any, although drinking an unspecified substance in a house of ill repute was probably not a wise decision on my part. As for the whores, there's no judgment here. After more than 4200 gigs, I have certainly become a bigger whore than that honey in the headband.

MY FIRST PAID GIG

My first paid gig differed greatly from my very first gig. Yeah, because of the pay, which was $25, but there was more to it. We actually rehearsed for my first paid gig. We promoted it. We wrote up a set list. I changed my guitar strings. I approached the date with some seriousness.

The act was an acoustic duo in which we both sang and played guitar. We had a pretty extensive repertoire for being such a young band. I was 19 and it was my first real musical endeavor. The "brothel" band from my first gig only knew a handful of songs. In the duo, we had a song list of about 60 songs, mostly Beatles and soft rock hits from the 60's and 70's.

We rehearsed a few times and got a gig at a local saloon in Westchester County, just north of New York City. I think it was called the Press Box because the owner was a writer for the local newspaper. It was really small, holding no more than 30 people. I remember pulling up to the gig that Thursday night and being stunned by the amount of cars parked in front. Did 30 people drive 2 cars each?

The place was mobbed. All of our friends showed up to support us and drink beer. They were wildly successful on both counts. I was nervous to be singing in front of people for the first time, but I got through it with the help of a very friendly audience. We played every song we knew, the crowd sang along with us and the bar made a lot of money and asked us back for the next Thursday.

It was a great first step in my life as a professional musician. It was a tiny place, so it was easy to fill. There were no real technical problems as the PA was basic. We just set the speakers on the floor and plugged in. It was in the neighborhood, so we had the home field advantage and had the crowd on our side before we played our first note. In that one 4 hour gig, I learned to set up and sound check in a crowded room. I realized that making a phone call, using the bathroom and grabbing a drink all in a 20 minute break should be an Olympic event. I learned that even at this level, everyone wants your attention. It takes a lot of energy to shmooze with 30 people, each of which suddenly wants to give you an opinion of your band.

I got a lot of schoolin' from that first paid gig. It set the tone for many of the next 4200 gigs. My idea of conducting myself as a professional musician initially meant learning the songs and performing them and that was about it. Essentially, I thought I'd play the notes and sing the right words. End of story. It never dawned on me that there was a social aspect to being a pro. Offstage, I would be obligated to talk to all those people, receive that many compliments and complaints and have to smile all the way. Onstage, I learned to forge ahead and entertain under any circumstances. Even when strings were breaking and speakers were crackling, we could never let them see us sweat.

This was all made abundantly clear to me on that first night. On the surface, it appears that a gig would be all about me. After all, I'm onstage and I'm performing. It's actually all about them and I do mean all about them. It is your job as an entertainer to make every single person in the house feel as if you are playing for them. It's my belief that the entertainer should make the corner bar feel like the Coliseum and the Coliseum feel like the corner bar. Make the people in the smaller venue feel as though they are part of the greatest show on Earth. Make the huge crowd feel as though we're all sitting in the intimate settings of your living room. Make sure the pub crowd goes home feeling as though they have seen a band that is bigger than life. Make every member of the larger crowd know that you were looking right at them when you sang.

BOTTOM LINE:

Great! I was a 19 year old guy with $25 and the whorehouse had already burned down. Apparently, God has a sense of humor.

SET LIST VS. SONG LIST

A set list says a lot about the band. Some choose the latest TOP 40 radio hits. Others play jazz standards or country. Most wedding bands play a little of everything. If you are attempting to be a working club musician, start learning JOHNNY B. GOODE. Everybody says they know the song. They play it every night. Most play it wrong. Let me say that another way. WRONG!! Let's not take the time to dissect it now. (Call me at home. We'll discuss it then.) Do us all a favor and get a copy of the original recording. Promise me you'll listen to it. Get the original key, the tempo, the groove. Then go listen to 20 club bands play it. You'll be amazed!

The idea of playing the same old songs everyone else is playing isn't always appealing. Try to think in these terms. They're not the "same old songs." They're standards. They're classic tunes. Every band plays them because every audience loves them. Every audience loves them because these songs are hits. They are familiar. They are timeless. Honestly, there have been times when I have dreaded playing some of these classic standards. This is where professionalism comes into play.

Remind yourself that you are on stage to entertain. These people are here to dance and to listen to some good music. Find a way to make performing this song fun for you. If you can't put your personal taste aside for 3 ½ minutes to please the people that are paying to hear you, maybe you shouldn't be there.

The following is a list of 5 frequently requested classic songs:

Johnny B. Goode
Brown Eyed Girl
Mustang Sally
Twist and Shout
Sweet Home Alabama

Here is where we compare a set list to a song list. All the tunes you have chosen are appropriate for the rooms you are working. You have a good mix of oldies, dance and slow tunes. Now what?

You break this list into 4 sets of 10. A basic club gig is four 45 minute sets. It should be about 10 to 12 songs per set. Constructing a good musical set isn't always as easy as it appears.

You might need to play a cocktail or dinner set. This usually means a lower volume, lower energy set of material geared more for listening than crowd participation. A dinner set is common in restaurants where the dining room is still full at 9 PM. The dance crowd usually arrives at 10 PM. Your job is to make an easy transition from quiet dining to more of a club atmosphere.

This is the dinner set, not the LAME SET. This is not an excuse to solo for 8 minutes while the pianist makes a run for the Swedish meatballs. The samba version of Boogie Oogie Oogie might have your fellow musicians in stitches, but you really should do better for the sake of the audience. There are several alternatives.

Cole Porter, Miles Davis, the Beatles, James Taylor. So much of this music is timeless, popular and recognizable. It's also musically challenging. It can be extremely fulfilling to pull this stuff off and have people react, albeit in reserved fashion. Standing ovations are rare during the dinner set, but you'll be able to tell if you're doing well. A lower energy first set is where you can perform this type of material and showcase the band in a different light. The drummer can use brushes. The lead singers can stretch out and "croon" at this volume. You can make a great impression playing a cool dinner set.

The second set is the time to step it up. You are trying to keep the dance floor filled. You play some favorite disco and current dance. Remember to slow it down every 3 or 4 songs. Give the slow dancer -or in my case, the no dancer- a chance to shuffle his feet for 3 minutes. These slower tunes are usually a good time to bring down your volume. (More on the volume thing later) Allow each set to breathe. Make each 45 minute set a show. Arrange the set to appeal to the audience, not the band. Does the crowd need 4 sax solos in a row? An entire set of 50's? Is everything in the key of "G?"

Put some thought into it. Showcase the band. Spread the vocals around. Spread the solos out. The band doesn't have to suffer. Throw in an instrumental and let the drummer play "out" a little bit. He had to park 2 blocks away, for goodness sake! Show him some love! Use one or two segues so that "down time" is at a minimum. It doesn't have to be Holiday Inn shtick or Las Vegas glitz. It could just be a tight band putting on a good show.

BOTTOM LINE:

The idea of taking your song list and constructing a show is a chance to set your band apart from the rest of the pack. Done correctly, the band takes the crowd on a little ride. You can have the patrons dancing and screaming and then 10 minutes later, you have their undivided attention as you sing a ballad. The band is at the controls. The audience is having a ball. It's a win/win situation.

MY BAND PAYS BETTER
THAN YOUR BAND

Most working club bands are either classic rock or variety/wedding bands. I have met some of the most talented players in wedding bands. Really. The image of the tired old guys in powder blue tuxedos has done quite a disservice to this part of the industry. Some may question my use of the word "industry" when discussing a wedding band. Well, Potsie, let me sketch this out for you.

Roger, the sax player shows up at 5:30 for a 6 o'clock wedding gig. 4 hours later, he has played to 150 screaming and dancing partygoers. (Typically, that's about 135 more than you'll play for at your original gig at Wally's House of Fish.) After dining on rib eye and wedding cake, Roger arrives home at 10:30 with $300 in his pocket.

About that time, across town at your gig, your Mom is begging Wally to stay open because the rest of the family is on their way. "They really are party people. They'll pack the place!" God bless Mom. You consider your original band part of the music scene, but you have no respect and regard for the wedding band that is playing a mind- boggling number of tunes and styles, often transposing keys on the spot to accommodate different singers.

Let's face it; some of these wedding bands are pretty damn good.

BOTTOM LINE:

You may want to reconsider your position here. The variety band is a great training ground in many respects. It may not be the ultimate goal for you, but don't knock it. Many of those musicians are first rate. You should consider hiring a few of them for your band. If they're not busy doing a wedding for $300, maybe they'll say yes.

BUT, MY BAND KICKS ASS!!

The other side of this equation is the club band. A club band has the luxury of having some attitude. They can dress as they like. These bands can start late, play loud and drink beer. They play the songs they want to play and get phone numbers. They want to rock and roll all night, but wait, that's only the half of it. They also want to party everyday! These guys are so cool.

If you're in a club band, you're living the dream. In between cover tunes, you throw in a few original songs and the dream just got dreamier! You are having fun, making some money and you actually have an audience that likes the songs you write. This is the best of both worlds. You have found a way to get paid to play some of your material.

You play mostly bars. That's really OK. In fact, it's great. Bars are where real people hang out. No posing, no velvet ropes or guest lists. No VIP lounge. Real people throwing real darts and the occasional real bar fight. Damn, I'm getting homesick just writing this! Bars are where bands are supposed to play.

At around 9 PM…that means sometime before 10:30 PM, the jukebox shuts off in the middle of a song. It's very dramatic. The sonic void that is left is filled immediately by some random snare hits and some undefined noise from the stage. The singer grabs the microphone and before he can say anything, a guy at the bar yells, "Whooo!" That is the official start of the gig.

The first song begins and immediately, bikers, runway models and stay at home dads are all on their feet and having a good old time because of your band. You guys are making it happen. The crowd feels great and the band feels great. It ain't nothing but a good time. That's the way it's supposed to be.

ORIGINAL SIN

You want to play "originals," meaning songs you wrote. You really want to form your own band and play your own tunes to as many people as possible. Unlike the club band, you don't want to play anyone else's material. You want to make your statement with your music.

Good for you!

I think it's a great move. Nothing is more exciting than moving an audience with your own creation. It takes a lot of work. In fact, it usually takes more work than you ever dreamed. Still, at the end of the day, playing your own music is a thrill like no other. I did mention how much work it takes. Now, I'd like to take a little time to explain just how much work it takes.

Bad for you!

First of all, writing a good song can be difficult at best. There is no formula for writing a good song. Writing 10 or 12 tunes to fill a 45 minute set is quite an undertaking.

In a cover band, you simply choose the material and learn your parts. In an original band, each member is defining the sound of the songs. In many cases, these are the only musicians that have ever played these songs. Each member makes a unique contribution which shapes the sound. Often, no one plays the part quite like the guy who created it. That is the essence of a "band." Because of his musical insights and signature licks, a band member is absolutely irreplaceable.

Until he quits. Or gets fired. Or gets a better gig.

I wasn't trying to be funny, although I am hilarious. (I have the same problem with being cute. It's a curse.) Viewing a fellow musician as irreplaceable is common, but real world experience tells you it's not true. Replacing a player in a cover band is hard enough. Replacing

13

someone in your original band can be traumatic, but it's bound to happen. You'll get through it and you'll be fine. You'll find a new player and he'll be great.

It's important to look at the "new guy" as a tremendous asset. The newest musician in the band might be able to bring some different flavor and personality to the show. He or she might bring a little needed attitude to give the band some edge. Conversely, maybe the new player is more grounded and adds some stability to the usual chaos that occurs on a weekly basis during gigs, rehearsals and recordings.

All this new guy stuff is important in any band, but more important in an original act. Making the new guy feel welcome should be a band priority. Create an environment that allows him to use his talent to enhance the music, not just duplicate what the first guy played. Make sure he knows it's his gig now. He's not on trial. He's allowed to try a fresh approach to the music and make mistakes along the way. He's one of you. However, he's still the new guy, so make him load the van.

Keeping players on board in an original band is tough. Your band won't make much money. You'll need to rehearse more than a cover band. You'll spend a lot less time on stage. A club player gets $100 for 4 hours on stage. As an original act, you'll probably play a 45 minute set for free. That's the way it is and it's never going to change unless you work hard for a better situation. You have to earn it.

You will need to transform your original band into something that is so appealing that an audience will pay $10 to hear you do a 12 song set and then pay another $15 for your music online or on CD. This will require booking gigs, advertising, developing a following, all while you're writing and recording material you hope will be popular.

It's a very tough thing to do, but bands do it everyday. You have to get it in your head that this band is your statement that must be made. This musical endeavor represents your true self. Sure, you play in other bands for a number of reasons. One band is cool because it's all your friends, another band makes money. This original band is not a job or a hobby. It's a calling.

BOTTOM LINE:

Answer the call.

THE TRIPLE THREAT

I had the good fortune to be in a great club/wedding/original band for years. We were the ultimate triple threat. It was quite rare to find a band that did all these types of gigs. Those days were fantastic. We played 200 gigs a year, often playing 2 gigs per day on weekends. The money was good and the friendships were great. To this day, I am still good friends with all of those players.

The band was great for a lot of reasons. The talent was there. We had the typical 4 plus one, which is bass, drums, guitar, keyboards and a female singer. 3 of us were legitimate lead singers. Two of us doubled on both guitar and bass. The keyboardist played left hand bass when necessary. We had great chemistry and personality. Each gig was approached with a sense of both professionalism and humor. We had fun all the time, but we always did our very best to make the party unforgettable.

Our girl, Yassmin, was a tremendous talent. She was beautiful and a top notch singer/dancer. When she was not available, we hired her sister, Karmine, also beautiful and talented. Both went on to star in RENT on Broadway. Every member of the band had competent subs. On the rare occasion that someone subbed out on the gig, the band was still in great shape.

We were equally proficient at both private parties and clubs. Our song list was absolutely outrageous, numbering well over 900 tunes and covering the current dance tunes, 40's jazz, ethnic tunes, classic rock and disco. Unlike most other variety bands, we stepped outside the box a little and developed a reputation for peppering the cocktail hour with acoustic songs by Pink Floyd and The Who. The audience loved it, as it was out of the ordinary but appropriate for the setting.

We had the perfect gear, loading the entire set up in a station wagon. We became famous for setting up and loading out faster than any band on the circuit. We had to be quick because we usually had to get to another gig. Before the last set, I would move the car to the club's back door. At the end of the night, Yassmin would say, "Thank you! Good night." Somewhere between "ni" and "ght", the rest of us would unplug our instruments and start breaking down and loading out.

It was a beautiful ballet to watch. Barry, the keyboardist, was stage left. He would deftly reach up and unplug the PA speaker with his left hand while dismantling the keyboard stand with his right. Yassmin would wrap the mic wires while smiling and thanking the people approaching the stage. Herman would take the monitor, throw it on top of his guitar amp and wheel it out to the car. Guy was already on the way out the door with his 3 piece drum kit. Much of the time, he used only a kick, snare and hi hat. Accessories such as cymbals and tom toms were held in reserve for special occasions. I was stage right, making my way to the wagon with the speaker and mic stands to be loaded behind the seats. A 5 piece band was pulling out of the driveway in about 5 minutes.

On many of the 2 and 3 gig days, we actually had a road crew to move our stuff. We would set up and play gig # 1. Meanwhile, our crew set up gig #2 with our complete second line up of amps, drums and PA. When we finished job #1, we left immediately for job #2, where we could walk right in and play. Meanwhile, the crew went back to job #1, struck the stage and set it all up on gig #3. It was quite an operation for a local band just trying to make a living.

We also wrote some of our own material. In the midst of this hectic schedule, we found time to do some original dates in Greenwich Village, the Mecca of original music. These gigs were the times that we had the chance to play for ourselves as much as for the audience. After all, it was our music and we didn't get to hear much of our own stuff. It was a nice departure to play material that really meant something on a personal level.

BOTTOM LINE:

This band was a rarity, indeed. We had the talent, the contacts and the desire to play the local bar, the wedding at the grand ballroom and then the hippest club on Bleecker St. We were the original hybrid, predating the Prius and the Labradoodle by more than a decade. This was the band that showed each of us what we were capable of accomplishing. One situation made us popular, another paid the rent and the third allowed us to showcase our own songs. Each segment required some thought and attention in order to pay off. This taught me to respect every band and every musical situation. Now, at the ripe old age of 50, I no longer have to show anyone respect. That's why writing this book feels so good.

MY CORPORATE BAND KICKS MORE ASS SIMPLY BECAUSE WE MAKE MORE MONEY THAN THE WEDDING BAND. AND I MEAN A LOT MORE MONEY!!

I said you shouldn't judge your success by the amount of money you make.

I lied.

When you play for low pay and to a small audience, you tell yourself that it's all about the music. These gigs allow you to express yourself, bare your soul and speak your mind in a creative environment to appreciative, like minded people who dig your scene. When you play a monster corporate gig to 10,000 people for several thousand bucks, you tell yourself, "This is really cool." Then, you tell everybody else.

You don't always judge gigs by pay scale, but sometimes you have to admit that a lot of money is better than not a lot of money. I have turned down many higher paying jobs for cooler gigs which paid less. I have said no to $300 because my heart and soul was in the $100 gig. That being said, I don't recall turning down a $4000 gig for anything. My great buddy, E.B. has hired me for several huge annual corporate gigs. (We have been good friends for more than 12 years. These gigs have elevated him to "great buddy" status.) We have been hired by one of the biggest companies in the world for 6 years in a row. I won't mention the name of the company or the exact amount we received. I will say that the gig is totally sick. From what I am told, "totally sick" means "rather nice." I use the term totally sick, the younger members of the band think I'm awesome and my street cred is off the hook. Word to my mother, yo!

These corporate gigs are unbelievable. They sometimes last for 5 days. The band performs at conference centers, stadiums and arenas, often to more than 10,000 people. The band is great. We damn well better be great. We are flown to the gig, picked up by limo and taken to the nicest hotel in town. We are wined and dined and wined again by the executives of the company. We receive the royal treatment all the time, every time.

E.B. is often called upon to write material for these conferences. The band performs these songs and they become the rally cry of the event. We stand onstage and watch as our images are projected on huge screens. One show utilized 12 of these screens simultaneously. From any spot in the house, each 25 foot band member was easily visible.

After each performance, we sold CDs, signed autographs and posed for photos with the audience. On several occasions, we opened for some huge national acts. Each year, we end up backstage after the final performance with the executives already making plans to hire us the following year. It's always a thrill. It's a fantastic addition to my resume. It's totally sick.

BOTTOM LINE:

I have done other corporate dates in my 30 years of playing music. Most have been quite successful, with both the band and the audience being top notch. Many of these corporate gigs have been spectacular, but none come close to the E.B. gig. Not even close.

Remind me to send E.B. a thank you note. Maybe I'll ask Carmen Electra to deliver it. Naked. And drunk. Man, I really want to keep this gig!

YOU CAN'T MAKE IT
(you probably won't)

This is not meant to discourage you. This is a fact. The student body in law school and medical school is usually cut by ¼ by the second semester. The same is true here in music. Not everyone is cut out to be a working musician. In fact, most people are not. The hours, responsibilities and wages are unusual. To be truthful, the "weeding out" factor is far greater than that of law school or medical school. Most students hang in there for 4 years. The overwhelming majority of musicians fold up the tents way before that.

Here is a simple model of a typical situation in the average week of the common musician. (I use words such as simple, typical, average and common to lull you to sleep. Then, I decapitate you with the cold hard facts. Man, this is fun!) For the moment, we'll assume that we're analyzing a 4 piece band that does original gigs, club gigs and weddings. It is the same 4 players on each gig.

A club musician in LA or NY will probably do a wedding for $300 on Sat, a small bar or restaurant on Thursday for $100, an original 45 minute showcase gig for $50 and an unpaid rehearsal in the same week. That's $450 for about 12 hours work. Right?

Almost.

I've been in bands in which the members made $300 per gig. The band was tight and organized. We knew all the necessary material. Our song list was almost 1000 tunes. Rehearsals were for running through some new songs, finding keys and rehearsing backing vocals, and could be done in a living room, saving time and money. The band was a well-oiled machine. It was easy money. A time/money breakdown for this "tight band" would look something like this:

Wedding - $300 —4 hours
Club gig - $100 – 4 hours
Original gig - $50 –1 hour
Rehearsal $.0 -3 hours
Total=====$450 -12 hours

However, I've been in several other situations where a band was just getting started. The new band was not in as much demand and could not always command the same money. Also, 2 weekly rehearsals were needed. The new band did not have the luxury of a casual vocal practice in the living room. They needed full band rehearsal time. Rehearsal studios cost money that band members had to split.

The "new band" needs separate rehearsal time for the wedding and original material. The band splits the expenses of both rehearsal studio dates. We're not finished yet. You need to learn the entire repertoire needed for the wedding band. This requires at least 75 songs. You may know some of the tunes, but you have a lot to learn. That's another 10 hours of homework time that you need to spend.

A time/money breakdown for the "new" band would look something like this:

Wedding - $200 —4 hours
Club gig - $100 – 4 hours
Original gig -$50 –1 hour
Rehearsal (2) $0 – 6 hours (3 hours each)
Homework$0 – 10 hours
Total === $350- 25 hours

An average rehearsal studio costs about $20 per hour. 2 three hour sessions totals $120. Splitting that evenly among 4 players comes out costing each band member $30 per week, leaving each musician a total of $320 per week.

The "tight band" might very well play 3 weddings and 2 club gigs in a week for a total of $1050 per week, while the "new band" struggles to get a gig. That can be inspirational or frustrating to the new band. You hope to be in demand soon, but now you are starting to realize it takes some work to get to that level.

Let's take that model week of $450 for 12 hours. If you did that for 52 weeks, your yearly income would be $23,400. The newer band would make about...let's see, where is my calculator? Oh, they make less, alright?!? (This is 2009. Make any adjustments for pay increase and cost of living for the next 5 years. The point is still the same.) $23,400 is not big money for a full-time job. It's not enough to feed a family of 3. It is, however, a nice part-time income for a job that you love and that most people want.

BOTTOM LINE:

As previously discussed, money is not the only measure of success. You love the band. You love the feedback form the audience. You go to the music stores and check out the latest guitars and amps, particularly the ones that you can't afford. (Trust me, that won't change.) You realize that a sore throat keeps you home from your day job as a shipping clerk, but a compound skull fracture won't keep you from the gig at the corner bar.

If you are able to pay the bills as a musician, good for you! You're in the minority. The fact remains that many give up after a short time because of the instability of the job. The odds are against you. Will this fact motivate you or intimidate you? Time will tell.

DOS, DON'TS AND "JESUS CHRIST, WHAT WAS HE THINKING!!??"

Rock n Roll has been around for 50 years. It will be around forever. Rock music shocked the establishment with long hair and distorted guitars. After those elements became "mainstream", the public was introduced to cross dressing, blood spitting mutants who destroyed their instruments onstage. It's getting tougher and tougher to have "shock value" as a musician.

Elvis wore leather pants. Iggy Pop threw himself through glass. Kiss did the make up thing. David Bowie did…Iggy Pop…at least that was the rumor. Anyway, it's all been done. By all means, be creative, be cutting edge and all those other clichés. Just don't forget to be a musician. If you can play and sing and write cool songs, the multi-colored Afro and the codpiece will just be icing on the cake.

Now, in many cases, the aforementioned multi-colored Afro and codpiece would be imagery enough to make a simple point about shock value. I say thee nay! That's why I've gone a step further in order to enlighten you. What can I say? I'm a giver. Here we go!

Dream sequence 1:

Your band is doing the first original gig at the newest Hollywood club. You've rehearsed, you bought a new amp and the keyboard player's girlfriend is inviting all her sorority sisters to the show. You've all decided to wear basic black, the clear rock and roll answer to any fashion dilemma.

You each have a copy of the set list which has been rehearsed to perfection. The club is crowded. The musicians all give each other a high five and walk out of the dressing room. 1 minute to showtime. There is definite excitement in the air.

Suddenly, the side door swings open. An uneasy chill fills the room. Out of the smoke and dust of Sunset Blvd. steps the lead singer, wearing a lime green cowboy hat and no shirt. His plaid pants are- there's no other way to say it- the plaidest pants anyone has ever seen. How could he? We all decided to wear black!

It gets worse. Much worse. The singer, Rex Sharkskin, takes the stage and begins showering the audience with rose petals from a salad shooter. (Rex Sharkskin, a.k.a. Eberhardt Fahnsworth. Yeah, the stage name is a no brainer!) While unveiling the latest steps he learned from an internet dance studio, he begins to sing a capella a song he wrote in the waiting room at the free clinic that afternoon.

Your eyes dart to the corner of the room, searching in vain for a cigarette smoking Rod Serling to narrate this awful event. "I can't believe this is happening on the biggest night of my life. Rex has ruined everything." The sound of your own scream awakens you. This has all been a terrible dream. This could never happen in real life.

OH, YES IT COULD! And it does, all the time. In an attempt to do something "fresh" and new, a band member shocks the band instead of the audience. This horrible miscue usually throws off the band's equilibrium. The band's attitude onstage changes dramatically. Everything is suddenly a little off. The players feel embarrassed by Rex. The audience is laughing at Rex. The down spiral begins. The band feels it. The audience feels it. Thus, the biggest night of your life is ruined. Can this all be because of a stupid outfit?

Yes. More to the point, because of the stupid singer wearing the stupid outfit, singing that God forsaken song, all while attempting a dance that should only be done in the privacy of one's mind. The fact is there was a basic agreement as to what was expected of each player. It was a reasonable, amenable list of dos and don'ts based largely on common sense. Some of these items were discussed, others implied. The wardrobe issue was discussed and finalized. The set list was agreed upon and printed out. Rex ignored these items and decided on his own to go in another direction, resulting in a train wreck of a gig. When a band mate is in violation of these types of agreements, he needs to understand the ramifications of his acts. He must pay for pizza after the gig.

BOTTOM LINE:

Some of these little stories are funny and goofy. The point is serious. A band needs direction in musical style, lyrical content and fashion. A band is not necessarily a democracy. Someone has to lead. That does not give the leader the right to do whatever he wants.

The element of surprise is a gift to the audience, not to a player's ego. There are a million ways to present something fresh and new in a show. Just present it to the band first and think it through together. Your intentions might be good, but some ideas can easily backfire. You should test run some of these ideas before you're on stage. Work out the logistics in the rehearsal studio. If you don't, the downside could be huge.

STANDING ROOM ONLY

This should piss a lot of people off! Here is a rule of thumb for most working musicians in most situations. If you can't fit your rig in the trunk of a Jetta, buy a smaller amp. The amp, a gig bag containing wires, mics, etc. and a music stand should fit in the trunk. The guitar, bass, or keys can go on the backseat. The mic stand goes on the floor directly behind the front seat. Why am I so adamant about the topic of gear? (I said adamant, not Adam Ant. Lordie, you 80's folks drive me crazy!) It's simple. Room in the car is akin to room on the stage: It's at a premium.

The overall space the drums take up, known as the footprint, is usually the largest. You wind up competing for the remainder of the stage. The less room you need, the easier on everyone. Space is limited and inches count. Unless you happen to be a member of Cirque Du Soliel, it may not be easy to hang from the ceiling in order to fit the keyboards on the bandstand. Amps these days are compact, powerful and durable. Most have casters for easy transport. Most weigh less than 75 lbs. The stage will be easier to set up and maintain when using smaller gear.

Your choice of amp may be different when playing the Forum. Your favorite vintage stack may be the only thing you ever use when recording. What we're addressing here is the blue collar player. You pull up to the club 45 minutes before the gig. The closest parking space is 200 yards away. If the gig is in New York City, the closest space might be New Jersey. You need to set up quickly and efficiently. You probably have to move gear through some tables and chairs to get to the stage. I hope this is starting to make sense to you. Don't think of using a smaller amp as sacrificing sound. It's simply more practical and easier on your back. I like to think I've coined the term "chiropractical."

Amps are not the only offenders. Guitarists who feel the need to bring 4 guitars and put them all on stands onstage need to be slapped around. Hard.

Hey, String Boy. We don't doubt that your goal is to get that authentic, vintage sound which can only be duplicated on that particular vintage guitar. We know this because you explain it to us night after night. Meanwhile, the guitar museum that you have onstage is taking up so much room, the singer has to set up his mic off stage and the sax player has to stand on the toilet in the ladies room. There must be an easier way. Of course there is.

Shoot the guitarist.

No argument there. Still, there may be another way. Here's a thought.

Play your favorite all- purpose guitar and keep another axe out for a back up in the event that you break a string. If you suddenly need a third guitar, leave the stage and give the bass player the only solo in his 4 years with the band.

While we're in this zone, if your effects pedals outnumber the audience, try to consolidate. We all understand that these pedals are a big part of your sound. However, I have yet to meet the fan that said, "Wow, I'm bummed. I drove all the way from Poughkeepsie just to hear Johnny Turbo use his trademark FLANGO-VIBRATO-ECHO-OVERDRIVE –TUBE- PRE- AMP-METAL CHORUS, but it turns out he forgot his vibrato pedal and his overdrive is in the shop. That means he'll only have the FLANGO-ECHO-TUBE PRE-AMP METAL CHORUS. Man, it's just not the same."

I have all the respect in the world for a drummer. Even a small kit requires a lot of work to cart, set up and break down. However, I do tend to lose sympathy when he deems it necessary to use a 9 foot gong to play the Elk's Club Awards dinner. You get the idea. Each member of the band needs to address this issue. Don't be such a stage hog. Figure it out. Your sound and gear should be an enhancement, not a concern, to the band.

BOTTOM LINE:

The mo' room, the mo' better.

I AM THE SUN AND THE EARTH
REVOLVES AROUND ME

Working musicians all share a commonality and that is that everyone in the audience wants to be you. You can talk to women you don't know without fear. Guys will buy you drinks in hopes of meeting some of those women you don't know. You eat at the club for free. The bouncer is suddenly your friend. You can park in the NO PARKING ZONE behind the club. This little world is your oyster.

Sadly, you're allergic to shellfish and this oyster will damn near kill you.

You see, all this small town fame will undoubtedly go to your head. It always does. Every night at every gig, you are the rockstar/ladies man/prince of the city. When the sun comes up, everyone else realizes that this is a façade. When will you realize it? You better be careful. We all know your band kicks ass. Make sure it doesn't kick your ass. We all think the world of you but please keep your ego in check.

Having 100 people clap for you 3 nights a week can be a powerful aphrodisiac. If a few people recognize you on the street, your ego can inflate faster than...a musician's ego when he gets recognized. You know, I just could not think of a better example. Certain personality types are susceptible to this illness of getting high on one's self. Someone with self esteem issues, starving for attention and something to prove to his peers fits that mold. That profile fits many musicians.

The stereotypical cocky musician is an easy character to envision. He walks into the club as if he owns the place. Every gig is of the utmost importance, as many industry people will be in attendance. Producers, promoters, publishers and several other music executives that start with the letter "P" are knocking down his door. He talks about his band as though it's the greatest show on Earth, except no one ever brings him back down to Earth. He will crash into terra firma on the first of the month when the rent is due. It is then that this leader of the best ass kickin' band in the land realizes he has to call home to borrow money. He'll no doubt use his girlfriend's phone, as he has used up his pre-paid phone card.

If he's doing 3 gigs a week, he's working hard. He's just not necessarily making a lot of money. Of course, Cocky Boy's fans don't realize this because he talks about his band as if they'll be the next big thing. They assume he's doing fine when, in fact, the 21 year old secretary he's hitting on is in a higher tax bracket. He takes plenty of time to detail his band's exploits and career path. That is why each set is short and each break is long. He usually spends more time promoting than actually performing. Every now and again, a fan will ask why the band is still playing the corner bar. "I've been to every one of your gigs for the last 18 months. I've never seen any of these music big wigs show up. Are things really going so well?" The cocky musician will never let on. He will keep up this façade forever if necessary. He'll continue to talk the talk. God bless Cocky Boy.

Then, there's Complainer Boy, the other musician who is always bitching about his band. It's all he ever talks about. Often, this musician has a few friends that live vicariously through him. It can be comical to observe this scenario. The friends are on the mailing list and show up faithfully week after week. Complainer Boy talks to them week after week, complaining that the club doesn't advertise enough and that the singer shows up late. His "regulars" lend a sympathetic ear. They try to ease the pain with some kind words, but Complainer Boy doesn't know how to accept a compliment.

These fans are fully involved in the drama. They sit at their favorite table and talk to each other in hushed tones. "Can you believe that Frankie, the new sax player wants to sing Free Bird? Everyone knows that's Bobby's signature song. I'm so upset. I didn't sleep a wink last night!" These fans gravitate to Complainer Boy. Apparently, misery loves company and psychosis is always looking for a party.

Sometimes, a player gets to thinking and feeling that his band is the only thing that matters. The cocky guy can't wait to tell everyone how well the band is doing. The complainer is always telling everyone about the band's problems. In either case, these musicians have to realize one simple truth. You're in a friggin' bar band! The fate of the planet does not hinge on whether or not you are singing the right words to HEATWAVE. Enjoy yourself and stop making it sound so important. The band is good and we all enjoy having a drink and listening to you. Hey, Cocky Boy, your band is not as good as you think. Be thankful that we get up and dance. Now, shut up.

Not so fast, Complainer Dude. I have a few things to say to you as well. We came here on a Friday night after a tough week at work. I want to hear some good music. I did not come to hear you bitch and moan about your drummer's voice. I want to relax, not have a question and answer session with you. "Was I a little sharp on the bridge of that last song? The keyboards are too loud, right? I have a sore throat because I was on the phone all night with the bass player. He's going through a divorce, you know." My God, do you think anyone cares about this crap? Other than you and your overly involved fan base, nobody does. My advice to both Cocky Boy and Complainer Boy is shut the Hell up. Your stuff is not that important. Play your music and check your ego.

BOTTOM LINE:

Forget what I said. No musician ever keeps his ego in check. See you on Friday night.

IT'S PROBABLY THE WIRE

Many years ago, my friend Tom managed a music store in White Plains, NY. The store did sales, trade-ins and repairs on all musical gear. I watched as guitarist after guitarist brought in gear to be fixed. Each had their own assessment of the situation. "The speakers are blown." "I'm sure my pick ups are shot." "The power amp is fried." Without looking at the guitar or listening to the amp, Tom would answer. "It's probably the wire." He was usually correct.

Of course, there are a number of catastrophic situations concerning tubes, microchips, resistors and transistors that could possibly be at the root of the problem. What was often overlooked was the lowly guitar cable. You see, this $20 wire is the essential bridge from the $900 instrument to the $1200 amp.

You checked the wire twice, you say. I sympathize with you. You had some trouble getting signal in your fourth set last night. You tried to remedy the situation on the spot. As the band plowed on, you crawled around the darkened stage tracing wires and checking connections, thinking "now I got it" at every turn. You hoped the crowd didn't notice you down on all fours spewing foul language at an electrical outlet. These are not ideal circumstances under which to be a systems analyst. These circumstances are ideal for only one thing: Panic.

We've all been there. You're positive you did everything to check and double check the basic power flow and your chain of connections. Maybe. Maybe not. Consider this: Amps last a long time. Guitars usually last longer. Wires don't. That's probably why there are very few vintage cable shops in Hollywood. Can you imagine that pitch from that salesman? "So, you got your eye on that 15 footer with the 90 degree jack, eh? Clearly, you're a man of discriminating taste. This baby did the Ted Nugent World Tour in '75. It says $49.95 on the old tagger, but what the heck, the manager's at lunch. I can give it to you for $45 out the door."

There can be a substantial difference between cable manufacturers. The difference is often both in sound quality and durability. Many of us think nothing of plunking down big bucks for the latest guitars, amps and recording gear. When it comes to the cables, the electrical umbilical cord, we usually purchase the cheapest. Why? It's because we're morons. There doesn't seem to be another answer.

BOTTOM LINE:

It pays to spend the extra $11 on quality wires. It's also a good idea to take the time to wrap them properly when packing up. This prevents the wires from tangling and kinking. The extra 2 minutes at the end of a rehearsal or gig is well worth it. Most of us know this, but not all of us practice this. Show a little discipline in this area. It wouldn't hurt to throw a few extra wires in your bag or instrument case. The extra effort could save you some embarrassing moments on stage.

QUITTING THE BAND

You've come full circle. You did the audition, you got the gig, you've played with the band for 18 months and now you feel it's time to move on. You feel this way for any or all of the following reasons:

You're not making enough money.

You don't get along with one or more members.

You need to expand your musical horizons.

You're far more talented than the rest of the band.

You're far less talented than the rest of the band.

You're taking over your Dad's plumbing business.

You have made up your mind. You are no longer interested in working with this band. Do the right thing. Tell the band of your decision immediately. Do it the right way.

Get things straight in your head as to why you have made this decision. Be prepared to clearly answer some questions from your band mates. Often in these situations, the one quitting isn't comfortable talking about his reasons. For example, it can be tough telling the singer you think he's lousy.

You need to make yourself clear without being mean or insulting. It is within your rights to make mention of problems as you see them. You owe it to the band to be honest with them without being cruel. State your case. Give them at least 2 weeks notice. Be a professional and a gentleman and wish them luck. Let the band move on and get someone else.

This is important for all involved. You need to get on with your life. The others need to find someone to replace you. At the very least, that takes some phone calls. More often than not, it takes ads in the local papers, booking a studio for auditions, call backs, etc. The band can't afford to be out of work for a month trying to get a player up to speed. This is a business decision and should be treated as one.

It's not your intention to hurt the other players. However, there can sometimes be a feeling of resentment on their part. They'll say, "The band was just picking up some momentum. Now, we have to start over. It will never be the same." It's not your job to make them feel better, but in the interest of all involved, you should listen to what they have to say.

Offer to make the transition as painless as possible. Offer to help the new player. Send him a copy of any CDs or charts you may have that would help him learn the material quickly. Make yourself available to the person replacing you. Invite him to sit in for a few songs at the next gig. Introduce him to your audience. Make him feel welcome. Let everyone know that this is a positive step for both sides. In the end, the band will continue to work and you can pursue your career.

BOTTOM LINE:

Things can get ugly when someone quits the band. Feelings are hurt, income is lost and a lot of work lies ahead in order to replace a band member. There just might be an exchange of words. I've been involved in a few of these "exchanges" where there was more screaming than the birthing scene of Rosemary's Baby. I'm not advocating that type of behavior, but it is understandable. Everyone is putting their heart and soul and time and money into a musical project. Suddenly, one guy decides to leave and the project is compromised. It's a bad situation.

If you are the one leaving, you must consider everyone's feelings. You do what you need to do in order to move on. You might follow my advice to the letter but still get some flak from the band. That's life. Be a pro, wish them well and be on your way.

STARTING A BAND

I purposely put STARTING A BAND directly after QUITTING THE BAND because chances are good that you "joined" a band, got some experience and quit before you "started" your own band. You observed what the other guy was doing wrong and learned from his mistakes. Now, you have all the necessary tools and knowledge to venture out on your own.

Sure, start your own band. How hard can it be? While you're at it, grind your own contact lenses. Both endeavors can begin in your garage.

Clearly, I go a long way to make my point. That's what makes my writing so utterly delicious. I purposely put this chapter directly before the one called MY WORST GIG. I thought it would be a good primer and give you an idea of what you're getting into with this music stuff. I just hope it doesn't push you over the edge. I'll tell you again that the life of a musician is not for everyone.

Starting a band can be quite an experience. Your intention is to put together a few musicians to play music. That seems simple enough. You'll get together twice a week until the material is committed to memory by every player. When the band tightens up the necessary 40 songs, you'll book a few gigs at the local hot spots.

Let's hope so. Starting a band is akin to a high school science experiment. You take some basic elements and mix them together. Sometimes, you get the desired results, sometimes not. Once in a while, things blow up in your face. Sometimes, the singer is great but the bassist is a jerk. The drummer is a nice guy but can't seem to learn the tunes. Whatever the case, you started the band so you need to fix these problems or else!!

If you are putting the band together, make sure you are the one who has some leverage. Do you have booking contacts? Do you own the PA? You will need a carrot to dangle in front of the other players in order to entice them to be in your band. This is a new project with no track record. You need to have something to offer immediately.

This can easily conjure up the chicken and the egg question. Which comes first, the band or the gig? It can be difficult to get musicians to learn songs and rehearse twice a week with no jobs in the foreseeable future. It's much easier for you to get players to commit to your project if you have some gigs booked. Upcoming work will always motivate a new band to hunker down and rehearse, but how do you get these gigs without having a band? Who will hire your pre-embryonic band that only exists in concept? How do you convince a club owner or booking agent to hire a band that doesn't yet exist? When is a band a band? Is it at the point of conception or at the playing of the first song onstage? Suddenly, starting a band sounds like a terrible idea.

Don't give up. There are several ways to get started. You might want to start out small as a single or a duo to get some experience and solidify some relationships with club owners. If you start out doing a good job playing piano at happy hour, you might ask the owner if he would be interested in hiring your new band for one night at a reduced rate of pay. He already knows you can play and sing. You have been reliable and steady, so he could be willing to take a chance with the band concept.

You can also look around town at some of the other acts. There are always a few players who want to do something else. They might not be ready to quit their existing rock band, but they've always wanted to do a jazz trio on the side. They just haven't had the time to put it all together. That's where you come in. You do the leg work and plug in the right players. You handle the business and these guys just show up and play.

Another way to get a band started is to hire some players and record a video. This "virtual band" only exists on this video, as you never did a gig previously. You got together and recorded 8 songs and now this video will be distributed in your promo pack. If you get some bookings, hire as many players from the video as possible. If none are available, put a whole new band together. We've already established that it's easier to assemble a band if you have gigs to offer, so this shouldn't be too much of an issue. Be prepared to do some fast talking when the club owner asks why the band looks different. Many times, the first gig is a few months after he watched the video. Chances are good that the guy was drunk and doesn't remember much of it. Whew! That was close.

Starting from absolute scratch with 3 or 4 players with no experience is by far the toughest route. It's your first step on a very long journey. This often starts out as a garage band. You learn about music, gear and personalities, all before Dad comes home and needs the space to park his car. If you have a Dad that is willing to park in the driveway, you're ahead of the game.

BOTTOM LINE:

Starting a band can be quite a chore. There can be a lot of days when you take two steps forward and one step back. Don't be discouraged. The garages and basements are the laboratories where every band starts. Make sure you learn your lessons while in these labs. These lessons are invaluable.

MY WORST GIG

Long ago (1981), in a galaxy far, far away (White Plains, NY), I did what I can only describe as the worst gig of my life. I can try to make this story sound funny and entertaining for the reader, but the fact of the matter is that it was a miserable situation for a band.

My 5 piece band was making a living playing cover songs in small clubs. After a few months, we decided to try to book ourselves in one of the bigger clubs. CLUB A had a packed dance floor and a line around the block every night. All the hot bands played there. All the beautiful people hung out there. At least, that's what we were told. I had no firsthand evidence as we weren't a hot band and I only became beautiful much later in life. In short, I had never been to the club before we played there.

We phoned the owner in November and got booked on a Friday night in December, agreeing to bring 50 people in order to get paid $400. The club was bigger than any of our usual venues, so we decided to hire a sound company to supply us with a sound man and a large PA. We took the next few weeks and promoted the show as heavily as possible.

The big day arrived. We set up all our gear at 4 PM for a 9 PM start. The sound man arrived with a huge PA. We took the next 45 minutes running wires and setting up drum mics, all in anticipation of a night that would take us to the next level. We were ready to soundcheck when the sound man said he forgot something and needed to leave. He said he'd return in 30 minutes.

This was no problem for the band. We sat back and relaxed and had a bite to eat. We made a few last minute phone calls to check on our family and friends, double checking directions and showtimes. We wrote and rewrote the set list several times using up as much nervous energy as possible.

30 minutes became 90 minutes and the soundman was nowhere to be found.

We became worried at 7:30. The doors would open at 8. We couldn't start the sound check with all the beautiful people streaming in through the velvet ropes. Just before panic set in, the soundman's van screeched up in front of the club. We thought our troubles were over. It was then we heard the sirens.

A lot of sirens and a lot of lights. We had no idea what was going on outside. I ran outside in the freezing cold. There were 200 frigid people waiting to get in, many of which were our crowd. They don't know that the doors can't open until we do a sound check. The band doesn't know why the sound man isn't inside with us. Nobody knows why there are 4 police cars outside.

One of the police officers enlightened us. Apparently, our sound dude decided to go home to get some much needed illegal drugs. This is why he didn't return for 2 hours. When our illustrious hero realized the time, he grabbed the remainder of his cocaine and jumped in his van to come back to us. He ran 2 red lights and was speeding when the police tried to pull him over. He refused and a chase ensued. This pursuit ended in front of CLUB A about an hour before showtime.

It gets better. One of the bouncers tried to talk to the police on the band's behalf, explaining that this really isn't the band's fault and that all these patrons shouldn't be punished for this coke snorting moron's actions. "Let's get the sound man to finish his job of setting up the PA and then you can take him to jail." Now, I have no idea what the officer's answer might have been, but at that moment, the sound man started to resist, smashing the side view mirror of the van with his fist. He was handcuffed and taken away.

We were left to try to figure out the monster PA system. We failed miserably. We tried time after time to start a song. We blew fuses and had horrible feedback, all in front of a packed house. We let the DJ play some dance music for 30 minutes and we tried again with the same results. The owner came out and told us to go home.

It got worse. We couldn't pack up and get our equipment out through this crowd. We couldn't just leave all our friends who showed up for this special night that was supposed to get us to the next level. We were stuck here. Now, we had to face our fans and explain in great detail what had happened. We were humiliated again in front of all these people. It was then that my sister mentioned that there was a $15 cover to get in. 15 bucks just to get in? In 1981? Are you nuts? I thought I was having a bad night. Now, I'm looking at all these friends who stood in the freezing cold and paid $15 to watch a high speed chase, a sound man get handcuffed and a PA blow up.

Hey, when I put it that way, it sounds like a pretty good deal! Wow, this has been an awakening for me! After all these years of feeling guilty, I realize that we provided an abundance of entertainment for those ice covered individuals. I am free of these shackles. I am absolved.

THE MUSIC WORLD'S MOST OVERUSED PHRASES
OR
HOW CAN I SAY YOU SUCK WITHOUT SAYING YOU SUCK!

You poor thing, you really think your band sounded great. Tsk tsk... Wait a minute. I wasn't even at your show last night. In fact, this page was written on May 23, 2008. I couldn't possibly know what transpired at your gig a mere 12 hours ago. Am I psychic? Do I own a time machine? Am I the smartest man in the world?

The answers are no, no and, well, I like to think so. Sorry, Ace. It's time you took a lesson in Musical Cryptography and Colloquial Decipherability. Your first assignment is to figure out what you just read...take a moment...ok, let's proceed.

I will do my best to interpret some of the most common language you will hear directly after you walk off the bandstand. As with all matters in this book, I will do my level best to handle this with the delicacy it deserves.

SOUNDED GREAT OUT FRONT=you sucked

THE BASS PLAYER WAS SOLID=he sucked

THE MATERIAL IS REALLY COMMERCIAL=it sucks

GREAT STAGE PRESENCE=don't sing

THE CHICK SINGER IS AWESOME= I want to have sex with the chick singer.

Just for fun, read that again out loud and really fast. It's hysterical.

Be realistic. All your friends are trying to be supportive. They know how excited you are about your new band. They are truly happy for you. They drove 20 miles in the rain and paid $14 for cheese fries and a glass of something brown just to give you an audience. You come running out of the foot lights and say, "So, what did you think? Did you like that last tune? Don't you love the new drummer? You know you can tell me what you really think."

Right about now is the moment of truth. Your college roommate, Uncle Tad and J.J. from shipping & receiving all look you right in the eye and start using words like "amazing" and "awesome." Then, as if scripted, comes a stream of the previously mentioned over used phrases.

Hey, you had it coming. Asking these people how they liked the show is similar to your girlfriend asking you if she looks fat in that skirt. The truth? You want the truth? Every Jack Nicholson fan knows the next line. No one wants to crush you. No one has the heart.

Except me.

BOTTOM LINE:

Bad shows are going to happen. There will be any number of reasons for a bad show. Sometimes it's the soundman. Sometimes it's technical problems. Every once in awhile, you have to face the fact that the band just wasn't up to the task.

In reality, the good shows will far outnumber the bad. You have to learn from the mistakes. You have to trust your ears and instincts. Be analytical. Take the time to record or video several of your shows. Dissect the set. Be prepared to take some criticism. Choose your words carefully when critiquing your bandmates. Be open to making the appropriate changes. Be willing to rehearse these changes. You can't always rely on your close circle of friends to tell you how well you're doing.

Dear Diary #1,

It is October 18th, 2005. 2:15 PST. I just returned from a great gig. Some friends of mine play at HOWL AT THE MOON in Universal City in Los Angeles. It's an interesting place. It's a club that is centered on dueling piano players who take requests all night. These guys know a million songs in every key. They're quite remarkable. There are usually 4 core players, all of which sing and play piano, drums and guitar.

They have people get up and sing in a sort of "live karaoke" situation. Some of the local musicians sit in from time to time. I stopped by for a few hours.

I had the time of my life! The players were great. I had never met several of the players before. I was immediately treated as a member of the family. They were generous with their time and even more so with their compliments. They invited me to sing. They even made room for a few bass solos. We played some old favorites and then I followed on songs which I had never before heard. It was song after song with singer after singer, all the while players changing instruments without a glitch. At the end of the gig, each of the players asked for my business card. It was an extremely rewarding experience.

I felt it was important to include tonight's experience in this book. I was hanging around my house doing nothing that night. I was too lazy to get off the couch. I was content to spend the evening watching reruns of something. Anything.

It was then that I started recalling some of the points of this book. I remembered my own words. I remember my manager saying, "Gigs are your life's blood." I recalled writing that you can learn something from every gig.

I took my own advice and headed out for an unplanned, unrehearsed gig for which I would receive no money. It was a ton of fun. It was good for my soul. I handed out a lot of cards. Maybe I'll get some work out of it. Maybe not. If nothing else, it was a great way to spend a Tuesday night. I was doing what I should be doing. I was playing music.

THE ENCORE

Encore-

1. Again; once more
2. A demand, as by applause, for a repetition of a song, act, etc.
3. The performance or selection given in response to such a demand.
4. The chance for a band or performer to blow an otherwise successful gig by playing much too long just because their frat brothers yelled "one more."

What a fantastic night! You just played a set of your strongest original music. It was a harmonic convergence. The people who said they were coming actually showed up. The singer was sober, the soundman was paroled early and the van only broke down twice. The bassist remembered to play that elusive B flat on the bridge of song #4. The club owner gave you the thumbs up. On a night like this, saints preserve us, IT REALLY DID SOUND GREAT OUT FRONT!! The audience is yelling the single most anticipated word; ENCORE!

The mere thought of the word brings froth to an entertainer's mouth. It doesn't take much. A hint. A whisper. It's like blood in the water to a Mako shark. Someone at valet parking across the street said, "I wonder if they'll do an encore." The drummer heard that "encore" word, loud and clear. Our fearless drummer, Igor Smash (a.k.a....wow, that's his real name!), who is so deaf he can't hear his own complaints about the selection of beer on tap, heard it. His response was that of a terrier in a fox hunt. His head snapped so sharply to the left, he dislocated his ankle. In fact, he dislocated the sax player's ankle. I'm talkin' head snap, baby.

Igor alerts the rest of the band that an encore is imminent. They huddle backstage for a moment to decide on a plan of action. They all agree. "Let's play those 5 new songs we wrote last night. It'll be great!!" Yes, it will, for you guys. Not for the rest of us. Remember that "giant sucking sound" that Ross Perot talked about in 1992? Brace yourself. Here it comes.

Shortly after encore # 3, the people you once held in the palm of your hand are getting restless. They are feeling betrayed, actually. They showed their support and approval. They thanked you in the most genuine way an audience can thank an act. In return, you abused them. You overstayed your welcome. They stayed for the first song out of joy and appreciation. They stayed for the next 2 out of a feeling of obligation.

BOTTOM LINE:

This was supposed to be an encore, not an "on and on and on and encore."

The fans showed you that they love what you do. Give them the show they deserve. Do an extra song to end the show and exit gracefully, leaving the crowd wanting a little more. They'll get more of you at the next show.

VOLUME CAN BE VERY LOUD

Ah, volume, my pet peeve. I have never seen a more divisive issue than volume. Every band is too loud. Every musician thinks it's the other guy's fault. The guitar player starts explaining that his amp is only 65 watts. The singer needs more monitor because she can't hear herself over the drums. Terms such as room frequency and standing wave are tossed around like beads at a Mardi Gras parade. When anyone from the audience suggests turning down, they are hammered with the "you just don't understand" speech.

I'm not a real technical guy. I'm certainly no acoustician. I do maintain that if something is too loud, the remedy is to turn down the volume. You can say that to a plumber, an accountant and a bus driver without getting an argument. For some reason, asking a musician to turn down is immediately construed as an insult and therefore met with great resistance. There is no clear reason for this behavior. You want people to enjoy your music. They want to enjoy it. They can't because the PA is so loud it blew off their eyebrows. The band has to understand that they have the wherewithal to make the situation better. It's called a "volume knob." In many cases, turning it to the left will often lower the volume, thus solving the problem.

If the band has the answer, why is there such a problem?

Why ask why? It doesn't matter. I won't generalize. Each musician is unique. It wouldn't be productive to analyze this. Not many would own up to being too loud. Too many bands are too loud most of the time. If you want proof of this, don't ask musicians. Ask the waitress who can't hear her patrons. Ask the customers who refuse to sit at the first 3 tables. Ask the club owner who loses money when customers walk out. They know it's too loud.

Let common sense dictate in this situation. If the band is playing loud enough to be heard from the back of a crowded room, how do think it feels to be standing up front? It's usually not a good idea to try to reach the back of the room. Some people are back there because they don't want to hear so much of the music. They may want to talk or socialize. Don't be offended. They won't stay there all night. When they're ready to dance or listen, they'll follow the bread crumbs and find their way back to you.

Here's a good rule of thumb. You play to the dance floor. The band should sound big and full half way down the room. The bodies (the audience) will soak up a lot of sound. Many small clubs are acoustically challenging. It can be difficult getting a great sound. Get the best sound possible, but not at the expense of the paying customers.

If you remember one thing from this book, make it this: Volume is the number one reason for being fired. It is your responsibility to play the room. That means you have to be a pro. You have to allow for the small venue. You have to consider the patrons. It is not the customer's job to make allowances for the band. If you're too loud, you're wrong.

BOTTOM LINE:

Any band will play a little louder when the energy is up. That's expected. There is a point of diminishing returns. Louder doesn't necessarily mean better. You want to reach the audience, not chase them away. Do you want to sound great to no one? It's like the old adage. If a tree fall in the forest… let's hope it hits the soundman. Do the right thing. Make the adjustment before you lose the gig.

…and to directly answer the question as to why a band can't seem to turn down the volume, the answer is simple. Bands are comprised of musicians. Musicians are morons. I thought I covered that already.

I'm not finished yet!! I know you're all thinking that your guitarist plays louder than anyone. You're wrong. The loudest guitar player on Earth is my good friend, Herman. Before you start vying for second place, that Silver medal goes to my other friend, Matt. Playing with both of them has caused me substantial hearing loss. That serves me well. Now, I won't be able to hear them cursing me for writing this.

MORONS AND IDIOTS

I wanted to give the reader a basic overview of the working musician, presenting each member of the band in a positive light. I quickly kissed that dream goodbye. The positive light angle never stood a chance. In addition, it's hard to get an overview of a musician because there are so many variables. Is he a multi-instrumentalist? Does she write her own material? Does the drummer have a signature sound? Is he a working player or does he just own a guitar? Musicians are much like the proverbial snowflake: No two are identical and they don't last very long.

We musicians are a goofy bunch, composed largely of morons and idiots. A few are talented and creative. Most don't have the IQ of a windsock. We're always running late because we're always doing something else that's really important. Our favorite movies all have the term "post apocalyptic" in the description or "Revenge of" in the title. We always refer to ourselves as musicians even if we never do any gigs. We don't call ourselves TV repairmen or waiters, although that's what many of us do for 40 hours per week. We call ourselves musicians. That's an unlikely scenario regarding any other job. "Hello, my name is Bob Jamison, CEO of Intelliworld Communications. We grossed $420 million last year. Of course, that's just my day job. I'm really a pole vaulter."

You can always tell a musician by the look in his eye. That's not a compliment. Look into the eye of a pro quarterback or a gunfighter and you see the steely glint of direction, confidence and purpose. A musician's expression is that of a trout on a hook. We are always surprised by life's consequences such as rent, bills and laundry. That's because we don't have the ability to think things through. Consider the following discussion which is being held somewhere in Hollywood at this moment.

"Dude, I just got this mint condition 1963 P-Bass."

"But, bro, how do you intend to pay for such an expensive piece?"

No, prob, dude. I put it on my credit card."

"But, bro. How will you pay off the credit card?"

No prob, dude. I'll sell my computer to pay off the credit card."

"But, bro. You don't have a computer."

"Damn..."

Dude and Bro better read this book immediately.

Despite all the aforementioned variables, I have taken it upon myself to encapsulate several player profiles for your edification. This is all done in severely bad taste with no regard for any musicians whatsoever. Enjoy!

DRUMMERS

Phil Collins once said the drummer is like the goalkeeper of the band. I don't know what the hell he meant by that, so I'll put it another way. The drummer is the most influential member of the band. You can't hide drums. Believe me, I've tried. They dictate the tempo of each song. The drummer is often playing every note of every song. He pushes and pulls the band, for better and worse. A good drummer can potentially save a band. A bad drummer will destroy the band. What makes a drummer good? A drummer will tell you it's a great sense of time. His fellow band members may disagree.

Don't get me wrong. A great sense of time is a fantastic talent. It has been said that there are 3 types of drummers; those that can count and those that can't. However, knowing the tunes is more important. Some signature fills need to be in the song, otherwise, it really isn't the song. Getting the all important "feel," that thing that you can't quite describe but which often defines the song, is as important as time. I mention this because I have come across far too many drummers who felt that their only job was to be the time keeper. They are sorely mistaken. If you are playing "Day Tripper" by the Beatles and you leave out those drum fills at the very tail of the song, you should be disciplined severely. NO PIZZA FOR YOU!!

The drums take up the most room on the stage and make the most noise. The drummer immediately has an identity, playing the world's oldest instrument which appeals to our most primal instincts. Start the second set with a basic drum beat and watch the audience react. The energy in the room goes up in a hurry. The girls start to dance, the guys start to pump their fists in the air and the drummer is elevated to more than just a guy in a black t-shirt. He is not just a drummer, he is THE DRUMMER. He's got the power. He's got the groove. He's the man.

Of course, he's still gonna ask me for gas money.

BOTTOM LINE:

This would be a good time to mention my great friend Christopher. He's a drummer that shows up at 7:30 for a 9 0'clock gig. He plays at a reasonable volume. His kit always sounds better than great. He sings. I am known for knowing "a million songs." Christopher knows 1.5 million. He's the best "wing it" drummer in the history of wing it gigs. He's a great guy with an incredible feel for making every song sound right, even if we're playing it for the first time. I've done over 250 hundred gigs with him and it's always been great. I suggest we clone him.

BASS PLAYERS

Bass: The final frontier. For the most part, a bassist is just a lousy guitarist who really wants to stay in the band. I know this because I'm a bass player. Being a singing bassist who has done an average of 200 gigs a year since 1985, I learned a few things about bass. I have come to the following conclusions:

1. Jaco Pastorius was the coolest.

2. McCartney is "it."

3. I'm not either of those guys and neither are you.

Learning from these icons is pretty much required reading for all bassists. The idea of trying to be one of them can be musical suicide. Most of us can't play as fast as Stanley Clarke. Few have the technique and flair of Victor Wooten. Even less of us will be as melodic and creative as Sir Paul. Here's a harsh reality: Even if you learn to play every bass lick from School Days, you're still not Stanley Clarke. What's a bassist to do?

There are ways to learn from the masters without memorizing Donna Lee note for note. Phrasing, tone, creativity and the always underrated "space between the notes" will all be helpful in any musical situation. These are all great lessons to be learned from the giants of bass.

I know this first hand. I am not a great player. I am not a technician. I couldn't cop some of those licks no matter how hard I tried. I did learn some of those other things. Those are the things that keep me afloat on a gig. I don't consider myself a great player. I do consider myself a good player who does a great job. (More on that later.)

I love it when bassists refer to their playing as "simple" and "solid." We all declare that it's "all about locking in with the kick drum and laying down the groove." Gentlemen, these comments are more than clichés. These are absolute lies and these lies are cries for help. Maybe our mothers didn't hug us enough as children. We need more spotlight! We are starved for attention. So, give us some. Is that too much to ask? We want to play fast and loud. We make believe we don't enjoy bass solos, but we're only fooling ourselves. We want 35 string basses, with 68 frets. We want to play way, way up the neck. We want sub-sub-subterrainean woofers driven by super duper mega watts. We'd get some notice then, wouldn't we? Let's see how pretty boy lead singer feels when we take the stage-nay, the world- by storm! Our legions of bass players all over the globe will undertake the long overdue overthrow of the musical community, one city at a time. My vision will soon become reality! We'll have our day, my people! I, Basszilla the Great, King of all that is low frequency, shall lead you to the light!!

…but in the meantime, keep it simple and solid. Wow, that was some cup of coffee I had this morning.

BOTTOM LINE:

Give a listen to Stanley Clarke's SCHOOL DAYS and Jaco's version of DONNA LEE to get a sense of true technical genius. Study any Beatle composition and realize that Paul McCartney is the master of making a bass line a major hook of the song. Then, come up with your own approach to make you stand out.

RARE SIGHTINGS SINCE 1990

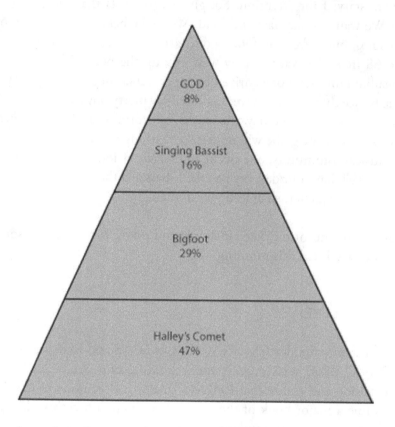

The above chart illustrates the sightings of God, singing bassists, Bigfoot and Haley's Comet between the years 1990-2009. These figures are the result of a poll taken of 100,000 people between the ages of 21 and 79. It should be noted that 2 of the 8% who claimed to see "God" were actually referring to David Hasselhoff after his kick ass show in Belgium in 1992. It should also be noted that 6% said Bigfoot was a solid fusion bassist, but like most jazz musicians, did not sing. 14% said they sighted Haley's Comet after overdosing on codeine at the 92 Hasselhoff concert. This seems implausible, as Haley's Comet has not visited the Inner Solar System since 1986. Less plausible is the concept that anyone would purposely dilute their kick ass Hasselhoffian experience by taking codeine.

GUITARISTS

Let's see. You play a Strat through a Fender tweed. Something is pierced. You put your foot up on the monitor every chance you get and you throw picks into the audience in hopes of getting that cute little honey's attention. THE HELL YOU DON'T!! I've seen you. We've all seen you!! Even when the waitress was digging the drummer, you struck a Whitesnake pose right in front of her.

There's a term for that, you know.

A guitar player can talk about string gauge until 2 AM. The person he's talking to usually falls asleep about 1:30 AM. That leaves the bartender about a half hour to sweep up before making the wake up call by jingling his keys.

Guitarists are a bloodthirsty breed. They will do whatever it takes to get attention. They'll stand in front of the drummer and the keyboard player. They'll play louder than the vocalist could ever sing. They turn an 8 bar solo into a 15 round prize fight, with the other band members taking turns trying to end the song. Guitarists are the Tonya Hardings of the musical community. Damn them all to Hell. That would be convenient, because I just got a steady Thursday night in Hell and I need a guitar player.

BOTTOM LINE:

It's widely accepted that most guitarists are not worth the time of day. As a guitar player, you should take steps to make yourself more valuable than the other guy. Singing is always a great asset. Playing another instrument will always make you more desirable or at least less fireable to a band. Spellcheck keeps telling me that "fireable" isn't a real word. Neither is Spellcheck, so piss off and let me get back to my writing!!

Brian is a gifted guitarist. He taught himself to play the banjo for one essential song in our set. He did the same with one mandolin song.

Brian doesn't consider himself a banjo or mandolin player, but we know he is, at least for those very important songs. He really stepped up big time and showed his talent and dedication by acquiring a new skill set. Now, we can't afford to get rid of him. I'm taking my cue from Brian. I hope my belly dancing is as readily accepted as his banjo playing.

KEYBOARDISTS

Melvin just sold 143 pints of his own blood in order to purchase the new VAVA-VOOM 3000 synthesizer. It has 64 drum loops, 12 helicopter samples and a lollipop dispenser. Melvin considers himself a keyboardist/composer. He is really an idiot/moron. He better read this before he gets fired/exiled.

Is it really necessary to have the newest keyboard? I think not. Is there a need to be constantly on the cutting edge of musical technology? Certainly not. Wouldn't it have been more fun for Melvin to make donations to the sperm bank and keep the cash? You make the call.

I'd like all the little Melvins out there to do the rest of us a favor. Put some time into working with whatever keyboard you own. Get a good B-3 organ sound and a few piano sounds first. Stop trying to keep up with the Jones' and concentrate on being a real musician. Learn to groove. Learn to be creative. Don't just get the latest product and think you've accomplished something.

Some of that other stuff is cool, no doubt. In the hands of a tasteful keyboard player, the sound effects, percussion and specialty sounds can really enhance a live performance or recording. In the hands of Melvin, the Zippity Do Dah patch will eat through your brain faster than the Ebola virus on black coffee.

HORN PLAYERS

You often overplay. You usually don't sing. However, you're usually the one musician who really knows how to read and write music. This means you're smarter than the rest of the band. We've already established that most of those guys are idiots, so don't let this go to your head. You own several jazz recordings, indicating you're very hip. When you talk about Cannonball Adderley, the lead singer's eyes glaze over as if he's going into insulin shock. "Yeah, I've heard of Adderly," says the bassist. "He played linebacker for the Dallas Cowboys, right?"

If you're a horn player, do yourself a favor. Get some sunglasses. If you wear sunglasses, people will think you play bebop. If they think you play bebop, they'll think you're really good. If they think you're really good, then it doesn't matter what notes you play. The audience will refer to all your mistakes as "jazzy" and "out."

BOTTOM LINE:

If you still suck, your only other choice is to wear a beret in addition to the shades. With these accessories, everyone will take your playing seriously and you'll save a fortune in lessons. Man, what a life!

LEAD SINGERS

The lead singer gets all the attention. The guitarist thinks he's getting the attention, but let's see who goes home alone after the gig. Lead singers are lazy. He (or she, or it) doesn't move any equipment. The LS has more time to hang at the bar during the breaks because he has no instrument to tune and no gear to tweak. He's the last one to show up at rehearsal and sound check. He gets equal pay. It must be wonderful to be a lead singer!

The facts are in. The singer is and always will be the most controversial member on stage. If he's good looking, the girls in the audience love him. This means the guys don't. If the lead vocalist is a girl, the guys in the audience love her and the guys in the band all want to borrow her hair products. The LS is up front, the first and last thing the audience sees. As the lead singer, you get cheered and jeered by the same crowd. Are you a copycat? Are you soulful enough? Are you as good as the last singer that fronted this band? It can be a lot to handle, even at the club level.

After all is said and done, cut the singer a little slack. Then, kick him in the shins. He still gets most of the chicks and we hate him for that.

BOTTOM LINE:

I often refer to musicians as morons and idiots. I fully acknowledge that I am a musician. Much like the court jester in a Shakespearean play, I attempt to cloak my serious point in humor, or at the very least, attempted humor. The serious point is that at any given time, all of us am idiots! When are we at our most impulsive, carefree and irresponsible? When we're in love! When we find love, time stands still, money means nothing and everything is possible. When you come to the realization that music is your true love, you are doomed to be gloriously idiotic for the rest of your days. Trust me. I know.

PIZZA

I really like pizza. If you don't, you should. Why am I talking about pizza in a music book? First of all, because it's my book. Second, it doesn't take much to get me started on the topic of pizza.

Pizza is the perfect food. It's nutritious, it's fast and it's inexpensive. It appeals to vegans and omnivores alike. It can be served as breakfast, lunch or dinner. If you haven't had cold pizza for breakfast, you're not a musician and therefore, I'll refund your money for this book. It's terrific before a gig or on a break because it's quick and easy. It's fantastic after the gig because…it's pizza, damn it!

It travels well. A pizza box can easily be balanced on the passenger seat without making a mess. Try that with chicken soup! It can be re-heated without losing its taste. It is easily augmented, as you can throw pepperoni, Gummy Bears and almost anything else on it and call it a "topping."

A rehearsal isn't a rehearsal without pizza. Before some Mama's boy talks you into sushi, take the bull by the horns and make the call yourself. Order at least 3 large pies. By rehearsals end, there will be a few slices from each pie remaining. Place the remaining pieces in one box. March the empty boxes to the recycle bin while the keyboardist plays TAPS. As you properly discard these dead soldiers, salute them for a job well done. They will soon be recycled and serve once again.

If you leave these left over slices in the car overnight after a gig, it stays refrigerated. If you leave it in the car during the day, it stays warm and ready to eat. I often travel with some extra mozzarella cheese in the glove box. Throw some on a slice and stick it on the dashboard before you head into the music store. In the time it takes to purchase some picks and strings, you've got some glorious "Za" baking under the glow of your windshield.

Damn, that's fine.

Always consider "pizza proximity" when booking a gig. Pinpoint the closest late night pizza joint. It makes the gig more enjoyable. After the third set, you stare at the clock, knowing that in a mere 60 minutes you'll be stuffing a glorious slice of cheese, bread, sauce and grease in your face. The anticipation of the pizza will be distracting. Sure, you'll make a lot of mistakes and the music will suffer. Some might say that is a lack of professionalism. I say it's the cost of doing business.

Now, if anyone has a gig in a pizza place, call me immediately.

BOTTOM LINE:

The chapter on guitarists contains 213 words. This chapter on pizza contains 469 words. Are you feeling me, guitar players?

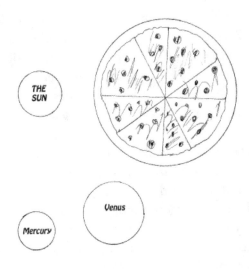

NETWORKING

The blue collar, working class musician looks at every personal encounter as an audition, an opportunity to meet someone who knows someone who can give your career a boost. You met a girl at your gig. She says she works for a record company. It's love at first sight. At your day job with the Bolshoi Valet, a car with the license plate MUZIC BIZ pulls up. You hope he hits you so you can hand him your video en route to the emergency room. You give a CD to your plumber because he's on his way to a big producer's toilet.

Admit it. We all do it. Hey, I had a waitress whose name tag read Mary Van Halen. I tipped her 700%. Most of the time, it gets you nowhere. What are you doing wrong? Isn't this networking?

Let's start with the obvious things. I would strongly suggest getting business cards. Writing your number on a cocktail napkin is no way to conduct business. A business card should have the basic info required. A phone number, an e mail address, a fax number and mailing address are all standard items. A list of your specialties or talents (drummer, vocalist, soundman, etc) should also be included.

Does any musician need a 7 color, 3-D business card? Probably not. They can triple the price of the cards. I have never done a thorough study, but I'll go out on a limb and say an extravagant card won't triple your business. I would suggest handing out 3 times as many simple cards to increase your exposure. However, a flashy card is another way to stand out a little. What the heck, I'm a big fan of self expression as well as self promotion. Definitely get yourself a card. You decide what it looks like.

Hand these cards out to everybody. Photos and promo packs are expensive. You need to be selective about who gets them. Business cards are inexpensive and easy to carry. Put them in your wallet, your guitar case and your glove box. Display them at your gigs. Never be without them. You can't let an opportunity slip away because you were unable to pass out your phone number.

PROMOSAPIENS

You have successfully handed out your business card and a few people have responded. They want to hire your band. They ask you for a promo package.

Your response will be, "Yes, I'll get it to you immediately." This poses no problem to you because you are organized and efficient. You are able to present your very talented musical act in a most professional manner. You simply go to your computer and send your EPK to your newest potential client. My goodness, that was easy.

Hey, you. Yes, you! Look at me when I'm talking to you! What do you mean, you don't have packages? You don't have promo packages? Are you familiar with the word "promotion?" You need to get on track right now. There's no time to lose.

You need photos. You need a one sheet cover page telling the client a little about the band. Mention what venues you have played recently. Include a song list. Include a DVD or video. This package will be pivotal in getting work for the band. You'll still do the occasional audition, but this package is your first impression, so make it a good one.

Putting together a promo package can get expensive and time consuming. Don't let that deter you. Get it done. It will be your connection to every potential client. Start with the basic steps that you can do at home. Write up a song list. Write a one sheet. A one sheet is a short (please, keep it short) bio on the band that tells the client where you are from, what type of music you play, recent gigs and so on. Include any other pertinent info and some recent photos. Get it started ASAP.

Since the dawn of rock n roll, bands have used flyers to promote themselves. In the Prepaleozoic Era, (otherwise known as the 90's) band members would print up flyers and hand them out, hang them on telephone poles and staple them to message boards all over town. This was always a lot of work. Most of the time, it was not worth the effort. Most people ignore pieces of paper stuck to light posts and stop signs. After all, most drivers ignore the stop signs, so it would stand to reason that the paper flyer stuck to it would go unnoticed.

Nowadays, the internet is the easiest way to get ignored…I mean, do some promo for your band. You can send electronic press kits (EPK). You can give a client your website address. Bands can email and text message their fans about upcoming shows. These methods are fast, easy and inexpensive. Fast, easy and cheap. That seems to be a theme in rock n roll. If you are cybernetically challenged and still don't have a handle on this wacky computer stuff, don't panic. Reach into your file cabinet and grab one of the many neatly stacked manila envelopes and address it. The U.S. Mail still works pretty well.

Bands still use the same idea of the age -old flyer on the internet. An effective flyer can be creative, but must have some basic info. Words like "TONIGHT" should not be used. (Can you guess why?) State the date and time clearly. For educational purposes, I will give examples of effective flyers and some not-so-effective flyers.

THE EFFECTIVE FLYER

THE KNUCKLEHEADS
@ Kravings
18663 Ventura Blvd.
Tarzana, Ca. 91356

Wed, Feb 3, 2010
Showtime: 8 PM and 11 PM
$5 cover.

THE NOT SO EFFECTIVE FLYER

The Bad Boys

Thursday at Perry's

We rock the house!

Party on!

THE WAY TOO MUCH INFO
FOR A FLYER FLYER

**THE BARKING
LOBSTERS
245 MAPLE ST.
Yonkers, NY 10705
914-555-3465
(Behind Jerry's dry
cleaners. If you get to the
gas station, you've gone
too far)**

Showtime is 8 PM, but we might
start a little late. You see, it's
my Aunt Celia's birthday and
I'm bringing the lasagna over
to her place in Secaucus, New
Jersey. Not a dressy affair, I'm
just wearing a nice shirt and
some slacks. Boy, my family is a
spirited group and the pinochle
can get pretty rough. Anyway, it
usually takes Aunt Celia a few
tries to blow out the candles.
This may cause me to run a few
minutes late. Traffic can be a
son of a gun, so we better make
showtime 8:30.

THE WORST FLYER IN THE HISTORY OF PRINT

I'll be over there.

TOURING: A VAN FOR ALL SEASONS

"Touring band" is a mystical term, indeed. What exactly is a tour? Is it a tour if you stay in a hotel after the gig? Do you have to drive more than 100 miles in order to qualify for tour status? Do you have to play more than 3 gigs in a row outside your area code? Even if it's not so clearly defined, touring sounds so professional. If a guy is on tour, he must be good. If a guy isn't on tour, well, he must suck.

Of course, this is not true. Touring is just a way to suck out of town! There is one major difference between a touring band and a local, stay at home band: The touring band can lie and not get caught! If you road dogs prefer, I'll say you exaggerate. Is that better, you lying sons of bitches? Here are a few basic examples of some of the son of a bitch-like lies that these sons of bitches might tell on any given night on any given barstool. In the spirit of full disclosure, I have heard (and used) the following phrases, usually in an attempt to impress women.

Tour Boy says, "We're performing at a theatre in Hollywood."

Translation: "We're playing a strip club in San Bernadino."

Tour Boy says: "The tour bus is great."

Translation: "the van has a cooler."

Tour Boy says, "The box office phone has been ringing off the hook."

Translation: "my mom called the bartender to remind me to wear a sweater."

Tour Boy says, "Doors are at 8. Showtime is 9."

Translation: "we start when the game is over."

Tour Boy says, "We did a meet and greet with our fans in the green room before the concert as per our contract."

Translation: "I had a beer with your sister before the second set."

Admittedly, a band on the road uses these phrases in order to sound impressive. You can't fault a musician for trying to sound impressive. Cut us some slack. We spend a good deal of our lives eating Corn Flakes and wearing the same socks for 3 days. Any chance to leave town is an opportunity to return with fantastic stories of huge crowds and huge paychecks. Local bands can't get away with that. They are forced to live with the harsh realities of small crowds, small paychecks and those socks!!

BOTTOM LINE:

You should tour as much as possible. If you want to see a prime example of a hard working band that tours constantly, check out my good friends, RAINING JANE. These 4 women are fantastic singers, songwriters, multi-instrumentalists and honestly, pretty easy on the eyes. ATTENTION, DUDES! These girls are like daughters to me. Mind your manners. If you're going to hit on them, be respectful. And it would help if you're rich. As I said, they're like my daughters and I'll need them to support me in a few years.

TEN REASONS YOUR GIRLFRIEND SHOULDN'T COME TO THE GIG

1. If it's a great gig, chicks will want to talk to you. She won't like it. Then, you'll have to endure that long, silent drive home.
2. She's going to hit on your drummer.
3. You'll make the mistake of asking her for an honest opinion.
4. She has been listening to you rehearse your slide guitar parts all week. When you screw them up, she's going to give you "that face."
5. You're required to pay for her burger and drinks.
6. She'll make the mistake of giving you her honest opinion. That's unfortunate because everyone but you realizes your band sucks.
7. You'll be self conscious the entire gig. She picked out this stupid shirt and made you wear it.
8. She'll talk to the other girlfriends who shouldn't be there. It doesn't matter what they talk about. It's not good for you.
9. You overhear talk in the men's room that she is 4 months pregnant with your drummer's baby.
10. She'll drink way too much and dance on a table. Then she'll make out with a waitress, which is cool except that the waitress won't go for the 3 way because she doesn't like you. Remember, your band sucks.

THE MAN WHO CAN'T BE FIRED

Rob was a drunk. Rob owned the club. That's never good.

I had a steady Friday and Saturday trio gig with Bobby and Billy, both great guys and phenomenal players. The club was usually empty and the owner was usually full of liquor. He was constantly complaining about the lack of business. Many patrons tried to explain to him that the place looked terrible and the food was beyond terrible. The drinks were overpriced and the service was bad. None of that mattered because Rob was a drunk and he owned the club.

One particular night in July, Bobby had to sub out. My good friend Herman, the loudest guitarist on Earth, was available to do the gig with us. It was an easy transition, as Herman and I had done hundreds of gigs together. Herman had moved from New York to LA the day before, shattering my record by getting a paying gig within 24 hours of moving across country.

We arrived at the gig and were greeted by a packed house. Drummer Billy's class reunion was in town and many of them decided to continue the party at our gig. Over 60 people showed up. As always, a crowd brings a crowd. Other people saw the line and all the cars in front of the club and decided to stop in. I introduced Herman to Billy and we hit the stage playing to a full dance floor. This had all the makings of a great night.

We ended the first set to fantastic applause. We were very pleased with ourselves for doing such a good job with a sub guitarist and no rehearsal. Billy was clearly the star of show. He was surrounded by 60 friends, many of which he hadn't seen in years. We took a very long break in order for him to say hello to that many people. To be fair, we did that 3 times. We took 3 very long breaks.

The night ended with thunderous applause. The room emptied with hugs and hand shakes for everyone. The waitress was grinning, as she made a killing in tips. The kitchen ran out of food. This place had done more business in this one night than in the last 5 days combined. These facts were obvious to everyone except Rob because he was drunk.

I walked up to the bar to get paid in usual fashion. The bartender was obviously uncomfortable. "Look, we have a situation here. Rob wants me to give you only half pay because you took such long breaks." Rob sat silently with his back to me 2 stools away. I confronted him. It got interesting in a hurry.

"Rob, what's the deal? Who cares about long breaks? We had the greatest night ever in this place. We brought all these people who ate and drank. They tipped well. They were a stupendous audience. I'm usually a "by the book" guy. I never show up late or take long breaks, but I think these are kind of extreme circumstances, don't you? Come on. Be reasonable."

"You get half pay for working half the night."

"Rob, that's ridiculous. We deserve a raise, not a pay cut."

"The Hell with you. Get out. You're fired!" As Rob yelled at me, he slammed his shot glass on the bar. I paused for about 3 seconds. Herman was all too familiar with these pauses of mine. History had taught him that it only gets uglier from here on out. Herman continued wrapping wires and packing up gear as fast as humanly possible.

I grabbed the empty shot glass and proceeded to pound it on the bar, accenting every syllable of my soliloquy. "Fired? Fired? I'm not fired! Let me tell you, you drunk son of a bitch. I'm getting full pay, right now. I'm getting full pay tonight and again tomorrow. I'll get full pay from you every Friday and Saturday night because I'm keeping this gig. Do you hear me, Rob? I'm not fired! I'm coming back tomorrow and there better not be another band on that stage. Now give me my money!" This went on for a while, but in the end, I was paid in full. I have no idea why that shot glass didn't break. I used a lot of syllables.

Herman had already packed up everything and we got in the car and began the drive home. It was stone quiet for a few minutes. My blood pressure was through the roof. I tried to calm down before saying a word. I finally said, "I got a little loud back there." Herman quickly said, "You really did. You were really loud." We both laughed.

The next night, I walked back in to Rob's club. I wasn't sure what to expect. There was the distinct possibility that I was fired. That should have crossed my mind before walking into the club, but it hadn't. That tells you something about me, doesn't it? There was a pretty good crowd, some of which were Billy's friends who were still in town. I entered the room to a standing ovation. Rob came over and said hello. I wasn't sure how much of our altercation he remembered.

People came up and started talking about the night before and how entertaining it was to hear me scream at Rob. How did they know about it? I thought they had all gone home before our "conversation" started. It turned out Herman was right. I was really loud. I was so loud that I was heard in the parking lot. Some of the old reunion pals saying good bye couldn't help but hear me screaming. They hung around for the festivities. I always dreamed that my voice would draw a crowd, but this isn't what I had in mind. Some quoted a few of my rants. I honestly didn't remember saying half of it. I tried to deny some of these, but there were too many witnesses. Clearly, I had said some really awful things to Rob in my effort to negotiate the extra $150. Apparently, I was persuasive, vulgar and hilarious. I was embarrassed, but only for a while. Rob didn't remember half of it because he was drunk and I didn't remember half of it because of my blind rage. What a pair!

Bobby will forever regret the fact that he subbed out that night. Herman will forever be grateful. Billy tells the story almost every night. To this day, I am known as The Man who Can't Be Fired.

BOTTOM LINE:

I was paid in full and we kept that gig for another 6 months, making this the greatest bottom line in the book.

BUYING GEAR

I have spent a lot of time and money in music stores such as Sam Ash Music and Guitar Center. It's easy to have a love/hate relationship with these places. It's always a thrill to see the newest, latest and greatest keyboards, loudest amps and vintage guitars. It can be tough to sit there and look at your favorite sax or snare drum and know that it's way out of your budget. You know this to be a fact because the last 3 purchases you made were way out of your budget. I hate it when that happens and it happens a lot.

The sales team is always eager to help you find any item. These folks work largely on commission, so they have a lot at stake with each sale. The more you spend, the more they make. They might have incentives to sell certain items. I never really have a problem with a salesman pushing a particular brand. After all, it's his job. It doesn't mean the product is of lesser quality.

Sometimes it's a new brand that hasn't had much exposure or an item that is overstocked. A sales pitch never stopped me from getting what I really want. The key is to buy what you really want and you should really want what you really need.

Shopping for musical instruments has never been easier. These days, you can do all your research online. You can research much more than prices. Look at magazine reviews of the product. Check out a few blogs and find out what the buyers have to say. How does the item hold up under gig conditions? Does the amp overheat when pushed? Is the lightweight cymbal stand as durable as advertised? In the case of a bass cabinet, you really want to look at the specs. How much does it weigh? What are the dimensions? What kind of dummy would buy an amp and wheel it out to the car, only to find out it won't fit in the car, no matter how hard you slam the trunk? I'll bet you think I did! Well, I didn't. I did, however, test drive a new car from the dealership to my house in order to see if my amp would fit in the car. I found an amp I really liked, so I decided to find the car that fit the amp.

You can be armed to the teeth with all the practical and technical info you need on any given piece of musical equipment before entering the store. You can always purchase gear online. I have done it without any problems, although I only shop online for certain items such as amps, cabinets and cases. I try to find the amp or cab in a store to check it out. Then, I go online to try to save money.

I usually prefer to buy basses and guitars from a store where I can actually put my hands on it and play it. "Identical" guitars can have distinct differences. One might sound a little darker. One neck might have a different feel than the other. I would rather not buy a guitar without playing it, so I do my research and then go straight to the music store in hopes of finding the deal of a lifetime.

At this point, you need to find your new best friend, the salesperson. He will tell you about the popularity of the product. "These pieces are flying off the shelves. We can't keep them in stock! You know that band REMNANTS OF PHLEGM? They bought 3 of these this morning." He will also tell you he's giving you the best deal he is authorized to give.

This is put up or shut up time. Are you going to stand pat on your final offer of $25 less than his lowest possible price? Are you willing to buy some auxiliary items such as strings, straps and drum sticks in order to negotiate a better overall package deal? Are you willing to walk away from the only guitar you ever wanted? Are you buying or flying? What will you do?

Relax, or as you young kids say, chill. Take a breath and remind yourself that you are in control. No salesperson can make you buy something you don't want, unless you're a guy and the salesperson is a cute girl. In that case, all bets are off. (Remember the new car story? The car dealer, Trina, was a Swedish gymnast. I have tried repeatedly to explain to my wife exactly why we now own 4 cars). Make sure you find a dude.

Remind the salesman that you are a long time, satisfied customer of his store. You would like to deal with him exclusively in the future. You want a solid business relationship. When you walk in that store for any purchase, big or small, you'll be buying from him. Then, make a final offer. If he calls you "bro," you're in good shape and you have a deal. If he calls you "sir", run for the hills.

If you are a girl, you will simply seek out the nerdiest salesman you can find. Not because I said so, but for the same reason geese fly south for the winter. It's because it's in your DNA. You'll twirl your hair on your finger. You'll smile sweetly and tell him that you need that keyboard so you can write songs about that boy who dumped you on Thursday. Now, you're single and alone. Within minutes, Nerd Boy will take out a personal line of credit, buy you the synth and deliver it to your house like the big, strong man he is!

Don't feel bad, Nerd Boy. Borrow my car. The trunk is huge.

BOTTOM LINE:

You have done your homework and you know exactly what gear you need. You know your budget and you know the price of the item. You knew all this before walking into the store. Don't feel pressured by anyone. You have all the tools to make an informed decision. Price is not the only factor here. Only you know how much this piece means to you. Sometimes, it's a good idea to pay $25 more than planned to have exactly what you want and need today.

SELLING GEAR

It might be more accurate to call this chapter "losing money" because that's exactly what will happen most of the time when you sell your used musical equipment. Basically, you bought something new, used it a few times and let it sit in the garage. Now, you want to sell it right away so you put an ad in the paper. You have decided not to trade it in or sell it on consignment because neither of these choices will get you the money you think you deserve. You tell yourself that there is a buyer out there somewhere who is willing to pay top dollar for this item. After all, it's barely been out of the house. It's as good as new.

Don't you just love it when someone says that something used is as good as new? That pitch never worked for me when I was selling toothbrushes. The buyer always wants a substantial discount on used gear, not because he doesn't trust you (although he doesn't) and not because he fears the item might be damaged (although he does) and not because he's broke (although we all know he is) but because there is no sense of security when buying stuff from a stranger with no warranty on the item and no sales receipt and apparently I'm in danger of writing the longest run on sentence in the history of print so I'm going to stop and try to regroup and choose my words carefully because this could get to a point where you, the reader, will begin to have trouble following my train of thought and then, well, then that will be a fine kettle of fish, won't it?

Used is never as good as new to the buyer. The expression "let the buyer beware" comes into play here. When buying used gear, the buyer takes all the risk, so he wants to buy low. The seller wants to sell high and tries to assure the buyer that the item is as good as new. The seller asks $75 more than the thing is worth and the buyer usually hides an extra 10 bucks in his sock. Now it gets fun. I will attempt to uncoil the twisted verbiage used in advertisements and negotiations that undoubtedly pepper these transactions. Here are some catch phrases used by sellers that require some explanation.

ALL SALES FINAL-I'm being evicted.

AS IS- it's disintegrating as we speak!!

MY LOSS IS YOUR GAIN- I bought this when I was stinking drunk.

GREAT DEAL- my Dad says I'm grounded until I sell this crap.

STILL IN BOX-please buy this before my girlfriend sees the charges on her credit card.

CLASSIC-it sucked 30 years ago.

RARE- only a few were made because no one wanted it.

VINTAGE- it's "burnt orange"

MINT CONDITION- I just stole it this morning.

BOTTOM LINE:

Unless you can get that cute girl to sell stuff for you, you're going to lose some money. So what? That's life! Sell the damn thing! It's just taking up space. The longer it sits, the less it will be worth. Get some cash and let the player who really needs it put it to good use. Take the loss and forget about it. Take the cash and buy another guitar, and do the whole routine all over again. Welcome to the club!

STOOPID!

Stuff happens. Even to me. I'm a bandleader who prides himself on attention to detail. I triple email and phone call directions and song lists. I take the band wardrobe to the cleaners. I deal with the club owners and book the gigs. Admittedly, I'm a control freak.

I would often catch myself saying to other players, "How could you get lost? I gave you the directions." "What do you mean you didn't learn the new songs? I sent you the CD and the charts." I looked at all of this as stupid. Just plain stupid.

So, one fateful day in Sept of 1986, I arrived a gig at a private school in the middle of Connecticut. That means it's a little rich kids school. The concert was in the gymnasium. Actually, the school was so snooty, we performed in the "James-nasium." At sound check, I reached for my trusty Ibanez 4 string bass. What I found in the case was my Fender Telecaster guitar! In my haste, I had grabbed the wrong gig bag when running out of the house. Here I was, bassless, 30 minutes before a gig. The 3 other band mates were not mad. They relished the moment. Here I was, The Gigmeister. Did I get lost? Did I forget to bring extra copies of the song list? No, I FORGOT MY BASS!!

I was embarrassed, I was humiliated. And I was rapidly approaching downbeat. We were 60 miles from any music store. I didn't have many options. I used the word "drat!" several times. I saw several 15 year old students having burgers in the cafeteria. I ran over to them. I was panicking. I asked, "Does anyone have any idea where I could possibly beg, borrow, rent or steal a bass of any type, brand or style for the next 3 hours?"

The 3 students looked at each other for a moment. The clock was ticking. The first guy spoke up.

"I have a jazz bass."

"I have a 63 P-Bass," said the second guy.

"My Music Man has ultra light strings, but you're welcome to it. Otherwise, feel free to use my Hofner."

Apparently, I was the only guy on campus that didn't have a bass. I borrowed a no name bass from the campus music room and got through the gig without incident. That was more than 20 years ago. No one lets me forget it.

OK, there are two lessons to be learned here.

God clearly smiles upon control freaks.

Triple check your gear, particularly on road trips. You might look stooopid if you don't.

There may be a third moral, particularly for band leaders. Leading a band is a tough job, no doubt about it. It's easy to get miffed at your band for any number of reasons. Learn to count to ten (although as a musician, you are rarely called upon to count to more than 4) before you speak up about what someone is doing wrong. If you spend too much time hounding the musicians about their faults, it will come back to bite you in the ...bass. You know what I mean.

I have a confession. I used to be one of those guys who really got on your case for not being responsible. I didn't always take the proper approach. My intention was to rectify a bad situation. I'm the leader, there's an issue that requires my attention and I'm going to deal with it as directly as possible. On the surface, that seems fine. It's not always. There are ways to let a player know he has to "step up" without chastising or embarrassing him. As a bandleader, be aware of not just what you say, but how you say it. My experience in Connecticut made me realize that everyone makes mistakes. Even...m...m....me. Or is it..I...I...I? I forget. Drat!

BOTTOM LINE:

Even the best of us can be crowned MORON FOR A DAY. When your day comes, have fun with the coronation. Know that it only hurts for a little while, but the lesson lasts a lifetime.

THE BAG

Never leave home without the bag. It is needed to carry all the necessary trinkets to a gig, including an on the spot repair kit. The bag is essential to any working musician. You will never regret having it with you. You will absolutely regret forgetting to bring it to a show. Here is a basic list of items to be packed.

-Mic wires
-guitar wires
-capo
-strings
-picks
-straps
-mics
-wire cutters
-3 in 1 screw driver
-Allen wrench
-duct tape
-tuner
-extension chord
-8 inch pizza (just wanted to see if you were paying attention)

A nylon duffle or shoulder bag usually works well. It has a few side compartments, so you can organize things in order of priority. Guitar picks and strings should be kept in one of the easily accessible outside pockets. When these are needed, you don't want to be fumbling around in the bottom of a duffle bag. Tools can be stored in another pocket. Honestly, I don't know how to replace pick ups or input jacks, but I still pack a few tools. Usually someone on the gig knows how to make a quick repair.

That leaves the main compartment for your neatly wrapped wires and your laminated, alphabetized sheet music. Make sure you clean your microphone windscreen with an alcohol wipe after each performance. Then, return the mic to its padded, custom fit case. I usually throw some potpourri in there in order to keep things smelling fresh…Oh, my. I think I've revealed too much.

You get the idea. Think in terms of being a musical Boy Scout.

Always be prepared.

THE SINGER/SONGWRITER
Or
That Girl in the Coffee House
Who Really Can't Play Guitar

Don't get mad at me. I'm just writing what you're thinking. We've all been to the local place with the little stage where a singer/songwriter just hit town and is trying to make a mark in the musical community. The singer/songwriter plays songs about her life. Very deep. Very emotional. The musical presentation isn't always what it should be.

No, it's not always a girl. I just wrote that to get your attention. There are plenty of horrible dude guitarists out there. I already admitted I suck.

In band situations, male guitarists outnumber female guitarists 100 to1. On the coffee house singer/songwriter scene, women are far more abundant. The band situation is usually an electric guitar rather than the acoustic guitar. Is electric guitar playing more masculine? Is it a male birth right? Is the long, sleek guitar neck a symbol? Could it possibly be an extension of a…you know…a boy's no-no place?

Isn't everything?

Bobby Riggs faced off with Billy Jean King on a tennis court in 1973. Riggs lost and the women's movement won that battle. Billie Jean King had made a resounding statement. However, most people admit that men are generally better at tennis than women. In fact, men are generally better than women at all sports. I think the same case can be made for guitar players. We can certainly name some fantastic female guitar players. Still, most guitarists are men. Why?

Here's my take on it: A female is attracted to singing while accompanying herself on an acoustic guitar because it is the easiest and often best way to communicate a lyric. Women are more in touch with their emotional side. More time is spent on the song writing than on instrumental technique. Thus, sometimes their guitar playing is suspect, while their lyrical content is more focused.

I'd like to ask all the feminists to refrain from throwing tomatoes until I've finished my point. I might surprise you.

Guys sit in the audience at these shows and criticize the girl onstage. "She plays like a typical chick. Her strum is weak. She insists on finger picking. She simply cannot play an F chord." I don't like admitting this, but it's true in many cases.

There is another truth here. WOMEN ARE SMARTER THAN MEN. That should have been the title of this chapter, but I wasn't smart enough to think of that when searching for a title. Hold on a minute! Maybe I should change the title now. Damn, too late. I already forgot about it. Oh, well...

I have worked with a lot of fantastic female singer/songwriters. It was usually a "less is more" situation. The band was often a low volume trio. The music was stripped down without a lot of bells and whistles. There were no elongated guitar solos. There was no goofy rock choreography or posing. No one begged for crowd participation. (So help me, if I hear one more lead singer ask me to throw my hands in the air like I just don't care, I just might throw him under a bus like I just don't care. And, believe you me, I don't care.) The songs were well crafted and both the voice and the song were showcased. The girl's guitar playing fell into the general category of "whatever," meaning it's not bad, but it plays a secondary role.

Some of these women play piano in addition to guitar, but they realize that pianos are heavy. Unless a piano is already in the venue, these women simply carry an acoustic guitar into a coffee house while across the street, their alpha male counterpart is hauling a 4x10 cabinet up 2 flights of stairs to play way too loud for people that don't want to hear him!

These women figured out a way to put their poetry out there with emphasis on the song, not the guitar solo. These women know that their talent and their music will grow steadily. They start with the basics: A guitar and a voice. The stage is small, the expectations are small but the experience can be huge. As the places get bigger, the audience gets bigger. This usually means more money. At this point, more musicians can be afforded.

Some men have figured this out as well. Men go the singer/songwriter route for a while, but they are mostly treading water until they get the opportunity to plug into a Marshall stack and leave that lyric nonsense behind. (Ah, I sense the slow, cautious return of the female reader). Women have found an arena that will give them equal opportunity. They have a more level playing field in the singer/songwriter community.

The women look at it this way: MOST musicians are idiots. ALL men are idiots. Male musicians, therefore, are the weakest link in the chain. Face the facts. There's more brainwave activity in a lobotomized Grizzly in hibernation than in most guys who play music. These women held a few private meetings-that's why they always go to the restroom in pairs-and devised a strategy to thrive in the cozy environs of the coffee house circuit. They have outsmarted the men and taken over a huge part of the music scene. The female singer/songwriter has evolved and adapted in Darwinian fashion. Right on, my sisters! Don't go quietly into that dark night. Lift your voice. Sing your song. Call me if you need a bass player.

BOTTOM LINE

I am not a chauvinist. In fact, I am very much a feminist. I have always loved the female singer/songwriter approach to a gig. The music is paramount, the melody is king and the lyrics are meant to be heard. I take those gigs every chance I get. I hope some of these girls call me. I know they're talking about me. I hear them through the bathroom door.

WORK TO DO

I was having a conversation with a famous manager. I'll resist the temptation to drop names but I will say he was one of the biggest managers in music. His acts were selling millions of records. We were discussing SLEEPER, my new band, which was becoming popular in the New York area. Admittedly, the band was probably starting to believe some of the hype. I was grumbling about playing low paying, local clubs, complaining that these gigs weren't worth the trouble. Big mistake.

Mr. Big Shot Manager stared me down until my retinas burned. I'll never forget what he said. "Gigs are your life's blood! You have to do gigs. You can't not do gigs." That was a long time ago. I repeat those lines every day.

Mr. Manager had acts doing world tours, TV shows and Rolling Stone interviews. He still saw the whole picture. He wasn't jaded by the fame or money. He made me realize that the "gig is the gig." Sometimes it's Madison Square Garden and other times it's in a hotel lounge in Tarrytown, NY. In either situation, it is your job to do every show with energy, passion and professionalism.

If you pay attention, you can learn something from almost any gig.

Very often, the last set on a Tuesday night can be very rewarding. The house is probably less than full. It might be a good chance for the band to stretch a little. STRETCH, not screw around. Play a tune you haven't done in a while. Take an extra solo. Let the bassist try his new slapping technique on a song or two. Do all of this in a constructive and creative environment. Maintain your professionalism. You're still on stage to entertain. The audience might enjoy you stepping out a little. This was the advice of Mr. Manager in 1987.

Since then, I've had the chance to play with band members of Elton John, Pat Benatar, Kenny Loggins, Michelle Branch, Jewel, Five For Fighting and many others. These players would have 4 nights off from their tour. They would come out and do a local gig with me for a modest paycheck. What I found fascinating was that these guys were always on time and prepared. Their attitude was great. They told me how much they appreciated the work. These players had incredible resumes. Their talent was evident. Yet, they approached my local gig with the same energy and respect as the bigger gigs. That is the definition of professionalism. That's why they get the bigger jobs. They understand that "the gig is the gig." Never forget that.

GREAT MOMENTS IN
WEDDING HISTORY

As previously mentioned, I have played in wedding bands. It was a tremendous learning experience in many ways. You were always playing music in a party atmosphere. The money was pretty good. Sometimes, the wedding was entertaining- even for the band.

Some of my fondest wedding memories have involved the best man. (Get your mind out of the gutter!) Ages ago, someone thought it would be a good idea for the groom to choose a "Best Man." One of the best man's duties was to toast the bride and groom, wishing them well on the road to eternal bliss.

Let's evaluate this for a moment. Somewhere, somehow, sometime, someone said, "Hey, Bob. I have an idea. You knew me for 10 years before I met Suzie. You were with me at 3 consecutive Spring Breaks. Why don't you drink a lot and then grab the microphone at my wedding!"

It's ridiculous. It's unbelievable. It's tradition.

I know we can all imagine all sorts of terrible things a best man might say. In my case, I don't have to imagine. I simply remember. The following toasts are real. They were all made in my presence. As I stood motionless and silent on the bandstand, the Best Man used my microphone to express his innermost feelings to the bride, groom and God.

The names are fictitious. The horror is real.

TOAST # 1.

"Thank you all for coming here to be part of the wedding of Mary and Paul. Paul, you are a fantastic younger brother to me. You're my best friend. Mary, Paul loves you very much. Even though the rest of the family refuses to accept you...I mean, he was engaged to Janet for 18 months and, well, she's a tough act to follow. Janet, can you stand up, please?"

TOAST # 2.

"Here's to Julie and Kevin. Hey, if it doesn't work out, just get a divorce. Cheers!"

TOAST # 3.

This one's a 3 parter!

The best man walks up to the bandstand with a quart of beer in his hand. I quietly asked if he wanted a champagne glass for the toast. He yelled, "Champagne? I don't drink that crap!"

Clearly having had too much to drink already, he proceeded to make the toast.

"To David and ...well anyway, I hope you two will be happy and have lots of kids. I hope your kids will stay in touch with you. Be careful, 'cause kids get weird. Look at my son, Joey. He's right there in the back with the blue suit. We haven't spoken for years. Look at you, sitting there. Would it kill you to say hello?"

We finished the gig a few hours later. As we were loading out down a flight of stairs, the best man approached us. He grabbed me with one hand and the keyboard player with the other. He pulled us close, all 3 of our faces almost touching. He looked as though he was about to cry. He had said some regrettable things earlier. I wasn't prepared for the next thing out of his mouth.

He burped. Big and loud and nasty. In our faces. There we were, trapped on a staircase with amps and guitars and a drunk spewing mushroom clouds of hops and barley through which one could barely see. I often refer to that wedding party as Til Breath Do Us Part.

This guy started the evening by proclaiming the champagne to be crap, moved on to forgetting the bride's name and finished off with embarrassing his estranged son. He was on a roll. That's one memorable toast. The burp was just a little present for the band.

There was one incident in which I was not involved. Not directly, anyway.

I was the bandleader on many weddings gigs. I was always on the gig. Everyone else subbed out, taking a vacation or taking higher paying jobs. I was always there. I decided to sub out on one wedding gig. I gave the agency plenty of notice. The band found a sub that fit right in. Everyone was happy. I had done my job by covering the gig and went to LA to visit some friends to enjoy my first weekend off in a very long time.

I returned to NY on Monday afternoon. I was well rested and ready to start my usual schedule of 6 gigs a week. I called Rory, the guitar player to let him know I had arrived back home.

Rory didn't even say hello. "Have you spoken to the agent", he asked. "No. I just got in. Hey, how about asking if I had a nice time in LA?" "You better call the agent right away," Rory insisted. "He's got something to tell you."

I was a little confused. I had only been gone 3 days. "If there is something to tell me, why didn't someone leave a message? In fact, if there's something to tell me, why don't you tell me right now"?

Rory told me what had transpired at the wedding on Saturday. Something ugly had taken place. I assumed the sub bassist didn't do a good job, but that was not the case. Our wedding band was a standard 4 plus 1, meaning 4 players and a girl singer. We had worked steadily for about a year. We never knew our singer had a problem.

On that fateful day that I decided to sub out, our girl, "Carla" (not her real name), had a fight with her boyfriend. She decided to have a drink or three. By the time downbeat rolled around, Carla was plastered. As the story goes, she began forgetting words. She started to wobble a little. In an effort to save herself some embarrassment, she left the stage. Her intent was to go to the bathroom and splash some water on her face. She only made it as far as the dessert table. Face first, as I understand. She fell into the table, knocking over the assorted pastries, cookies and ice cream. Thank goodness the wedding cake was on another table and escaped unscathed. In an attempt to stand up, Carla slipped on the spilled ice cream and fell flat on the floor in a slip and slide of hand rolled Italian canolis.

The band played on as they should until the groom approached and stopped them. The piano player assured the groom that this had never happened before and that obviously this gig was now a freebie. Carla then seized the opportunity to beg and plead with the bride and groom not to tell the agent for fear of being fired. Of course, they did and she was.

As I was being told this horror story, I couldn't help but feel cheated. I don't think I could have stopped any of that horrible stuff from happening. I just wish I could have been there to witness it! The laughing, the crying, the ice cream in the hair. Oh well. You win some and you lose some.

I've saved my favorite story for last. We were doing our typical wedding thing at a posh country club. It was a beautiful setting and a great party. Yet, it was all too typical to the band. We wore the same tuxedos, ate the same prime rib and played the same songs at all of these parties. Half the time, we couldn't tell which hall we were in because it all looked the same, smelled the same and felt the same.

I was set up stage right as always. While we were in the middle of a song, the bride came up and whispered in my ear. She requested that we play the classic Van Morrison song "Moondance" but not until she gave me the sign. I asked if she wanted me to announce the special song. She said no. I asked if it was to be played for the traditional "father /daughter" dance. She again said no, just to play Moondance when she gave me the green light. I told her we would be happy to do so. The band played another song or two and then she waved at me frantically to play her song. This didn't seem strange. After all, we had played hundreds of requests at hundreds of weddings. The bride wanted to hear her favorite song and we played it.

We took a break for dinner. As I was unplugging my bass, the bride approached me. "I can't thank you enough for playing that song." "No problem." I said. "It's our job to make your party as memorable as possible. It's our pleasure." "It really was special", she said. "Do you see that guy in the corner? That's Tommy, my first real love. Actually, we're still in love. I mean, marrying Jimmy is fine, but I need Tommy to know that no matter what, I'll always love him. Moondance was our song. I wanted you to play it while he was in the room. Even though I was dancing with Jimmy, I was smiling at Tommy. He knows I still love him." I really didn't know what to say. Imagine that! I was without words and that doesn't happen an awful lot. I smiled, nodded and walked to the band table to have dinner.

After dinner, the band played the big dance set, cut the cake, threw the garter and all the other typical stuff. In the middle of "Take the A Train" by Duke Ellington, the bride came up once again. I knew what was coming. She leaned over and whispered, "Would you play Moondance one more time"?

I smiled and nodded yes. We played it again and I watched as the bride danced with her new husband but had eye sex with Tommy from across the room. It was bizarre. There was this dirty little secret that only the 3 of us were sharing. While still dancing with her new husband Jimmy, the bride gave me a wink.

The party ended with a conga line and a standing ovation for the new bride and groom. The guests filed out and we began to tear down our equipment.

The drummer said, "Hey, what was up with the bride asking us to play the same song twice?" There I stood stage right with my head about to explode.

I huddled the band around me and began to whisper the story. "Everyone's gone. Why are you whispering?", asked the drummer. I began to tell the story again in full voice, with shrieks of "oh my God" and "that's unbelievable" from the band. That only led to a lot of off color jokes and really tasteless humor about the couple that just scampered off into wedded bliss.

As we blasphemed, a man in a tux walked behind me. "Excuse me, guys. Man, what a great band! I do a lot of weddings and I would love to work with you again. Hey, can I ask you all to step aside for a minute. I just need to get the video camera out from behind you."

I would like to take a moment to put things in perspective. This was 1987. Video equipment was big, heavy and expensive. Hiring a videographer to tape the wedding was just becoming commonplace, as not many folks owned their own video cameras back then. This videographer had one hand held camera that he used for candid shots. The other was placed on a tripod on the other side of a large potted tree. We never saw it. "We try to put the stationary camera in a spot where it can get a clear shot of the dance floor, but not be too visible. Otherwise, people come up and play with it, and sometimes knock it over. That's why I put it back here. It gives us a great shot of the room and the condenser microphone on this camera is great. You can really hear the band."

Did that camera pick up the bride's confession to me? Did it record me telling the band about her confession? What about those terrible jokes we made about the whole situation? I guess I'll never know.

My, oh, my. It started out as such a typical wedding.

I have tried to make much of this book witty and entertaining. I need the reader to understand that these speeches and situations really did take place. It was humiliating and embarrassing for some, humorous for others. I've been telling these stories for years. I find them hysterical. Of course, the parents of the bride may not share my feelings.

Now, class, what pearl of wisdom do we extract from this sacrilegious oyster? When all Hell breaks loose, the band needs to be cool. This is true on any gig. It's more true, truer, truest, in fact, the truthiest of all on a wedding gig. No other gig has the range of emotion, the social aspect or the religious significance of matrimony.

When these ridiculous people made these absurd rants in front of family and friends at $100 per plate, the band played on. I stared at my shoes. I bit my tongue. It was incredibly difficult, but under those circumstances, you simply cannot draw more attention to an already bad situation. You don't react to the best man's stupidity. You can't laugh and elbow your bandmates. You can't change what the best man has said, but you can do damage control. It is your job to get the crowd moving in a different direction, namely, the dance floor. Make them forget what just happened. Allow the bride and groom to believe, even for a moment, that the best man's transgressions have gone unnoticed. Do your job. It's all you can do.

Oh, and by all means, hold onto your comments until you all go to the diner after the gig. You never know who is listening.

MUSICIAN'S HOROSCOPE

AQUARIUS

This week, Aquarians will reach their creative peak. Money will be in abundance. Love is just around the corner. Sadly, you are an Aries. You're reading the wrong zodiac sign. God, you are such an A-hole!!

PISCES

Jupiter is in retrograde. Pluto got demoted. Mars is pulling you towards enlightenment while your wife of 11 years is pushing you out the door. Breathe deep and listen to the music of the planets. That probably won't help at all. Scratch that. Put some bourbon on your corn flakes and take a nap.

ARIES

Your sign is that of the Ram, named after the 9th Wonder of the Ancient World, the Dodge pick up truck. Since the Hellenistic Era, the Ram was able to carry nomads across the desert as they laughed at those morons holding on for dear life trying to ride those ridiculous camels. These street savvy Nomads could ride in luxury and comfort. Throw a cooler in that extended cab with plenty of cargo space, kick back and enjoy a few brewskis while observing the Southern sky through the moon roof, which is standard. Dude! These buds knew how to party, zodiac style. Venus is pushing you to buy a Dodge extended cab between the 3rd and the 17th, during the Dodge Ram-A-Thon when everything must go at low, low prices!! See your dealer today.

TAURUS

A water sign got your Earth sign all muddy. It's really hard to read. I think it says something like, GET A JOB.

GEMINI

The twins of Gemini will be in full effect from June 3 thru June 12, when you will realize your duality. On one hand, you will have to confront the side of you which is physically out of shape and financially ruined. On the other, you must come to terms with the goober in you that doesn't know his girlfriend is banging his step Dad. On June 13, things get bad. Best of luck with that gig on the 14th!

CANCER

You are born under Cancer. That never sounds good. You have the sign of the crab. Is that any better? Don't be a shmuck. Tell people you were born in October.

LEO

Mercury is rising almost as fast as your blood pressure. You're holding too much in. You need a release. Tell your night shift manager at Topiary World that you're trading in your chain saw for a Les Paul. In your hands, they will sound about the same. Buying a guitar at the age of 37 is a wise business move on your part, as guitarists are very hard to find in Los Angeles. You will feel totally liberated for 2 weeks, until you realize no one is going to hire you. You will come crawling back to the night shift manager who will do you a favor by rehiring you. Then, he will do the world a favor and take the chain saw to that Les Paul to make sure you can never play it again. All in all, I'd say it will be a pretty good month for you. The stars have been kind.

VIRGO

Monday thru Wed will be positive energy for you. Thursday will be meditative and enlightening. Friday will be joyous. Saturday will be a gift from the Universe. Sunday, you die.

LIBRA

It's October. It's raining. Your favorite baseball team is in last place. Spend the first 10 days eating cookie dough, the next 10 days watching soap operas and the 10 days after that being a guest on the Jerry Springer Show. On Halloween, dress up as the person you thought you'd be by this age.

SCORPIO

Mars is on your side for most of the week. You will enjoy great success in the stock market. The weekend just might surprise you as love may come in "threes." Then, Mars will come to collect, dispatching Martian troopers to abduct you in the middle of the night and probe you in places you didn't know you had. Small price to pay for that slammin' weekend. That's a great deal, my man!

SAGITARRIUS

The moon is in the 7th house. Your career is in the shit house. Call it a day.

CAPRICORN

The early part of the week should see some righteous solos. As you shred your way thru Jam Night, you'll meet a babe who will think your Members Only jacket is totally awesome. Oops, my bad. This is from 1984. Wow, I was just about do the Jane Fonda work out with Molly Ringwald.

REHEARSAL (A.K.A.
Practicing Your Mistakes)

Let's take a look at a typical band rehearsal. I say take a look, because we probably don't want to listen. Why don't we all just hold hands and jump in together!

Many bands simply don't get enough done in a 3 hour rehearsal session. Why? It's because the rehearsal studio is a place where the members of the band are left to their own devices. They are unsupervised and completely responsible for their time and actions.

They start by showing up 20 minutes late. Everyone figures the other guy is going to be late, so what the heck! The next step is to set up and tune up while talking about the traffic, Monday Night Football and the girl who does the band's mailing list. Before you know it, an hour has passed and nothing has been accomplished. And that's before someone orders a pizza.

Rehearsal studios are not always the best sounding rooms. Sometimes, the PA and gear are low quality or in disrepair. Get over it and get on with the rehearsal. Get around to learning the new songs. Fix the old songs that need some rearrangement. Decide on beginnings and endings. Address the musical problems first and foremost. Who's playing that funny chord on the intro night after night?

THAT FUNNY CHORD is the reason God invented the rehearsal studio in the first place. In almost every band, there is one guy who plays the same mistake every time. You all hear it, but you forget to mention it on the gig. You need to get this straightened out in rehearsal. These things take time. Too much time is wasted in the studio, therefore not enough gets done. I can hear you now. "Uncle Bill, how can we resolve this issue? We're morons and can't figure it out for ourselves! Please help us. Save us from ourselves, Uncle Bill!!"

I hear you, my fledglings. The answers are out there, but you won't like them because they are simple but can be oh so painful. Try not to flinch.

Take rehearsals seriously. I'm not saying don't have fun, but get down to business right away. It takes a lot of work to make a band sound good. Get there on time. Know your gear. Set up quickly and efficiently. Make a few notes before hand as to what you think needs to be discussed. Don't just play your favorite tunes. Make them all sound great and they'll all be your favorites.

Realize that there is no audience at your rehearsal. If you need to focus on one verse, do it again and again. There's no need to play the whole song. Strip the song down to bass and drums and identify any problem with the groove. Sing a cappella. Find which notes are suspect. Fix it, simplify it or drop it. Don't try to hide the mistakes with volume or energy. This could get a little embarrassing for the player who has been skating through the last few gigs. HEY, THAT FUNNY CHORD GUY TURNED OUT TO BE YOU!!

A basic 3 hour rehearsal could/should go something like this:

9 o'clock.

Load in and set up. Talk about a few of the songs that need attention.

9:20

Play a little for sound check. Loosen up for 10 minutes by jamming.

9:30

Get right to the point and address the mistakes. Go right for the 3 most problematic songs. Spend an hour if needed. Be particular. Get the phrasing of the vocals, not just the words and notes. Make sure the drummer knows about the very last hit of the song. Go over each problem area until all members are comfortable. Record those parts so you don't forget them an hour later. Any type of portable recorder will do. You're not concerned with the quality of the recording. Give them a listen the next day and commit them to memory.

10:30

Take a 15 minute break. It's not wasting time. It's necessary. Ear fatigue won't help anyone.

10:45

Run over the problem spots again. Then, play the entire songs in order to play the parts in context. Then, move on.

11:45.

Time to pack up. You need to be out by 12. Have some respect for the studio dude who opened the place at 10 AM and needs to get home. While you're wrapping wires and loading out, talk through a few ideas of what you want to accomplish next rehearsal or gig. Keep it organized and relaxed.

BOTTOM LINE

A well rehearsed band is always a thing of beauty to listen to and to watch. Practice at home is good for your individual performance, but a band is interactive. You need to feel the other players, not just hear them. Playing your musical role is essential. A simple musical part is no less important to the song. Playing a song with groove, feel and polish is incredibly rewarding. It rarely takes great technical players to make a great band.

NY VS. LA

I was born in New York City, New York. I lived in the New York area until I was 31. I then moved to Alabama for about 6 months, after which I moved to Hollywood, California in 1990. This circuitous route from coast to coast with a brief stopover in the Gulf Coast taught me a great deal.

I was a full time musician in all 3 places. I left NY in 1990 at 31 years of age for a woman in Alabama. (Don't be too judgmental. She's hot and we're still together after all these years.) All my New York friends couldn't believe what I was doing. "There's no music scene down there. All they play is country. You'll be bored out of your mind."

This became a point of debate for months. Each of these New York musicians had their opinion about the Deep South. None of them had ever been to Alabama. In fact, most had never been south of 14th St. Still, they were convinced they had very clear pictures of the music and the players. After all, it couldn't possibly be good in Alabama! "It's all the way down there!"

Being a native, I completely understood this attitude. New Yorkers see things as black and white. You're either a New Yorker or you're not. There are the Yankees and then there are a just bunch of other baseball teams. If you live in Alabama or Tennessee, you're a Southerner because you're down there somewhere close to Mississippi or Louisiana. Alabama might be very nice, but it's not New York. A Northerner is someone who lives in Vermont, but a New Yorker is a New Yorker. Period. Black and white. Against the advice of my friends, I moved anyway. After all, I'm a New Yorker and nobody tells me what to do, except this woman from Alabama.

I was visiting the music stores in the Mobile area prior to my moving there. The owner of the first store in the small town of Fairhope, Al. was wonderful, offering to pass my info along to anyone who might need a singing bassist. We shook hands and I pushed on to music store #2 where I met the rudest redneck bastard to ever stand at a cash register.

I introduced myself and explained that I was new to the area and looking for work. I would officially be living here in about 3 weeks and would appreciate any help making contacts. This ass looked at me and moaned, "Don't bother. There's no work down here." I smiled and stood firm. "Ok. I'll just leave you my card. If you come across anyone that might need me..."

"No use," he interrupted. I tried again. "But, all I want to do is leave my card. Just put it up on the bulletin board and leave it." No way," replied Ass Boy. At this point, a tiny bit of the New Yorker in me came out. "You know what? I came in here to introduce myself and give you my card to stick on your cork board. All I needed from you was a thumb tack and maybe a smile. I guess that's too much to ask." Ass Boy was already exhausted. "There's no work. I've been here for years. You won't get a gig." "Maybe not!" I fired back. "All you had to do was take my card. You could have stuck it on the board, put it in a file or thrown it in the garbage after I left. I don't know why you are making this so difficult." He moaned on and on. "There are no gigs. It's that simple. You won't find any gigs."

As Ass Boy was "Eeyoring" about the state of musical affairs in the region, a guy walked in the store to pick up some drumsticks. He tapped me on the shoulder. "Hey, my name is John. Did I hear you say you're a singing bassist? My band works 3 nights a week. That's our truck outside. We're on our way to Atlanta, but we'll be back in town on Monday. We're looking for someone like you. Do you have card?"

John called me and I auditioned the next week, got the gig with John's fantastic band RUMBLE HOUSE and played with them steadily for the next 5 months. We performed all over the South, including Pensacola, Fla., Birmingham, Al. and Jackson, Ms. Guitarist Joe would take center stage and energetically introduce me each night as being from "New York City!" The good natured southerners all shrieked, "New York City??" This ritual was great fun as it was usually followed by our spirited rendition of Sweet Home Alabama.

I got to thinking about that fateful day in Ass Boy's music store. Had Ass Boy accepted my card quickly, I wouldn't have stayed long enough to meet John, get the gig and ultimately be able to pay my rent. In the final analysis, Ass Boy was responsible for getting me the job. Funny how the universe works, huh?

On Sept. 13, 1990, I arrived in Los Angeles. On Sept. 15, I had my first audition. Most of my gear hadn't arrived in town. I had to rent a bass amp from a little place on Sunset Blvd in Hollywood. The salesman said, "Well, we don't usually do rentals, but I'll make an exception. You seem like a pro. A lot of you guys from New York are pros." On Sept. 17, I did my first gig in LA. The bandleader said, "Look, you pretty much had the gig when you walked in. I know you played 200 gigs a year in NY, so you have the job."

I was flattered at the time. I appreciated the break the salesman gave me. I appreciated the gig...for about 20 minutes. It was a horrible gig with a horrible drummer for horrible money, but it paid the rent. I still look back at those days with a certain sense of...horror. OK, I forgot my point again.

Oh, yeah.

It seems as though New Yorkers and Los Angelenos forget that there are 48 other states, and many of these states have musicians. Now, hold on to your hats, my friends. This is where sound check meets reality check. Are you ready? Some of these musicians are as good as the ones in NY and LA! And I'm not just talking about those Nashville cats, no sir. I'm talking about the 17 year old guitarist in Tulsa, the 45 year old drummer in a jazz combo in Maine and the 26 year old waitress in Walla Walla who finishes her shift at 9 PM and goes straight to rehearsal every Tuesday.

These folks in the "fly over states" are working just as hard as anyone else to hone their craft. Many are phenomenal musicians. It's ridiculous to think that musicality is based on where you live. Sure, where you live can influence your music. Cajun, classical, etc. Musical style is regional.

Talent is not. You are not automatically better because you play in Hollywood. Let me put this all another way: Anyone who thinks that musical aptitude is based along lines of latitude and longitude has an attitude with far too much altitude. Would that Sunset Blvd. salesman have made special concessions and rented me the amp had I been from Canada? I don't think so.

Of course, we're not done yet.

I learned some very valuable lessons in several different regions of the country. I thought I knew how to play the blues until I moved to Alabama. The guitarist kept telling me to "lay back." I wasn't sure what he meant. I wasn't playing too fast. I was just on the "happy side of the beat." It took a while before I could hear and feel the difference. I still struggle with it.

I played in a World Music band in Los Angeles. The material included Peruvian, Tejano, Salsa and several other Latin feels that were new to me. The musical director talked to me during the first rehearsal. He was smiling, trying desperately to be polite as he gave me some constructive criticism.

He essentially told me he appreciated my learning the material. He realized I had done my homework and had played the correct notes. However, my feel was that of a "gringo Holiday Inn band." He asked, rather, insisted that I be more authentic in my approach to Latin music. "Ah, Latin," I thought. "Very interesting. The language is dead, but the music lives on." One might say I had a lot to learn. I spent some time listening to some vintage Sergio Mendez, Celia Cruz, Djavan and Tito Puente. It was a humbling experience but a very valuable education.

BOTTOM LINE:

Realize that there is a global musical community. Make it a point to seek out new music, new bands and new musicians. Performing with some musicians who are 20 years older and others who are 20 years younger will give you a tremendous musical vocabulary. Playing with bands from other countries will help give you a broader musical palette. It will also open your eyes and ears and help break down some silly pre-conceived notions. Good music can come from anywhere. Actually, it comes from everywhere.

ARE YOU A GREAT PLAYER?

The answer is "probably not." Of course, these are the types of questions that start conversations that last long into the night. What makes a player great? Is a guitarist great because he can play fast? Is a singer great because she has perfect pitch? What if a guitarist is fast and has perfect pitch, but the audience just doesn't like what he's playing? Clearly, all of this is subjective. There are too many variables to get a straight answer, except that you're probably not a great player.

OK, now even more of the readers hate me. Shouldn't I be saying things like, "reach for the stars," "you can be anything you want to be," "practice makes perfect" or "always wear clean underwear." Yeah, like there's a musician out there with clean underwear!

You may never be a great player no matter how hard you try. That is not the end game. You should probably spend more time (maybe a lot more time) learning to do a great job. Earlier in the book, I admitted I am not a great player. I did say I do a great job in a band situation. I never had tremendous commercial success, but I have played on my share of indie CDs. I've gotten a bit of radio play and a number of TV and movie placements. I have secured an endorsement deal, thanks to my good friends at Warrior Instruments. None of these small victories had anything to do with technical skill. I have stayed on top of my game by working a little harder than the other guy. I focused on doing a great job.

Now, how does one go about doing a great job?

I would like make a real statement here. I need to say this from my heart in all seriousness. Your job as a working musician is to do everything you can to make your musical situation better. Here are a few examples of what you can do in order to do a great job.

Know the tunes inside and out. Don't just learn your parts. If you sing, get familiar with the low and the high harmonies. It will always be in your best interest to be aware of how the other singers are approaching their parts. It's more than just hitting the right notes. Where are they taking a breath? Are they hitting the first syllable harder than the rest? Get these things straight and you'll be amazed at the difference.

Dress the part. Make sure you look like you're part of the band. There are many bands wearing t-shirts and jeans. That's their image and that's fine. There are plenty of cool t-shirts to be found. I would suggest starting with one without coffee stains.

Be on time. Have a positive attitude both on the gig and rehearsal. Listen to what your band mates are playing and just as important, listen to what they are saying. Learn to take suggestions. Criticism is not necessarily an insult. Don't take it as such. Be a pro and learn from others who may have a little more experience or expertise.

Be patient. You might have the ability to learn your parts easily. Have some compassion for the guy who is struggling a little. Give him a little more time and space to get himself comfortable with the music. If he asks for help, you should be there for him. He might just need the extra 3 minutes to practice that riff in slow motion a few times, trying it in a few different positions on the guitar neck or keyboard. His frustration will most assuredly double if he sees you rolling your eyes because you feel he's taking too long to learn a simple phrase. If you feel this situation looming, step outside and grab a cup of coffee and let the guy do his thing on his own. It usually works out for the best.

See the bigger picture. Understand what you need to learn as well as what you have to offer. I know far too many players who practice 4 hours a day, but rarely play onstage. I know many others that are discouraged because they can't play some of the more difficult music that they love. I think both of these cases should be examined. If someone with great chops but no gig joins a working band with limited musicianship, they might all benefit. Mr.Chops could wind up being the musical director and get some practical experience about gigs. The other players can learn a lot from a schooled musician. If everyone involved understands what is to be gained, everybody wins.

Being responsible, internalizing the music, dressing appropriately and respecting your peers are all items that will help you do a great job even if you're not a great player. Of course, there are a million other duties to be done such as booking rehearsals, designing business cards and sending emails announcing upcoming gigs. I strongly suggest you do none of them. After all, that's your girlfriend's job.

BOOKING AGENTS AND OTHER
SINGLE CELL LIFE FORMS

Well, well, well. Finally, something upon which all musicians can agree: Booking agents suck. To be fair, I shouldn't lump them all together. I should say not all booking agents suck. That is tantamount to saying "not all pit bulls bite." If you are a booking agent, feel free to stick your arm in a pit bull's mouth to test this statement.

Most booking agents aren't musicians. They usually don't understand the needs and wants of a band. The agents seem to think that an additional hour on stage each night without additional pay is "standard." The agent often refers to a low paying gig as an "opportunity" and a chance to "get in on the ground floor." These booking agents are direct descendants of the slave traders. Shakespeare wrote, "First, we kill all the lawyers." Maybe we should make a package deal and knock off a few agents as well.

Clearly, I have an issue with these agencies. In fact, I have more issues than Sports Illustrated. Agents have lied to me. I have had signed contracts broken by agencies. When legal action was discussed, the agent made it clear that we would "win the battle but lose the war." In essence, we might get compensated for that particular gig, but we would never get booked again by that agency. I actually had a long time booker forge a band leader's signature on a contract, agreeing to less money, more hours and only 2 hotel rooms for 5 musicians. I actually saw the forged signature. I couldn't believe my eyes. As it turned out, I had to believe my eyes, but I still can't believe the agent. As a band, we tried reasoning with him. That was not at all productive. I should have followed my initial instinct to punch a hole in the crown of his head and use him as an umbrella stand. At least then he would have been of some use to me.

On the surface, you probably don't want to be booked by a company with such a lack of regard for the talent. However, sometimes in the harsh light of day, you realize you need these unscrupulous bastards to get work. This poor excuse for a human being is all you have and you can't lose him. You can't necessarily find another booker on short notice without losing a few months of work. It's a Catch- 19.8. That's a Catch-22 minus the agent's 10%.

I realize an agent should be compensated for his work. Contacts and relationships with club and casino managers have to be nurtured. An agent spends much of his day on the phone finding work for his clients. Many times, it's a thankless task. 10, 15, even 20% seems fair for a job that is paid strictly on commission. I understand it can be a tough line of work being a booking agent. I still say most of them can kiss my ass.

As a musician, you need to book as many gigs as you can on your own. This will give you a feel for what is required to keep a band working. You will realize how many phone calls and emails it takes and how much time and energy is needed. You may only need an agent part of the time. You may also realize that you simply aren't capable of that work. You aren't good on the phone. You don't have the patience to do the necessary follow up.

What else can a band to do? Not much, really. You don't have many options. It's hard to shop around for an agent. In reality, a band has to take what they can get most of the time. If the band does a poor job, they won't get booked again. When the agent does a bad job, he is rarely penalized. There are very few ways for a band to penalize an agent. Instead, you make a deal with the devil. You give up your sense of fair play and honesty. You take the work that the agent books for you. You do your best job as a musician and hope the agency keeps up their end of the bargain.

With any luck at all, you will become successful and outgrow that agent, only to be booked by a bigger agency and make more money. In this case, living well is the best revenge. And if you ever get the chance, find the first agent's address, put a flaming bag of dog poop at his front door and ring the bell.

Of course, I know there are honest booking agents. They have been sighted riding unicorns on the mythical land bridge known as Atlantis. I know this for a fact because the Loch Ness monster told me.

BOTTOM LINE:

OK, I know I've been tough on these agents. Relax, there will be no apology. However, I must list one AND ONLY ONE agency that has always shown their artists respect and consideration. I have done hundreds of gigs for Creative Music Consultants in Westchester, NY. Owner Ron Calabro was always a first rate guy with both a business and a musical background. CMC booked several of my bands from 1986-1990. After I moved to LA, CMC would occasionally hire me as a sub when I was in the NY area.

Ron and his staff were honest and forthright about every aspect of the gig. They took the time to give us advanced notice of any problems with an upcoming gig. We were always made aware of a difficult load-in, specific song list and special "guest singers" from the wedding party. These details made every gig, private or corporate, much easier and more organized. We were always paid fairly and on time. This treatment made every musician want to give a little extra. Each band understood that doing a good job was good for the band but doing a great job was good for everyone in the company. CMC treated us well and we rarely let them down. To this day, I don't understand why more agencies don't operate this way. Is it because Ron and his staff are incredibly smart and philosophically enlightened?

Hell no! I've known Ron for 24 years and he's always been a dopey bastard! C'mon, Ron. I've given you guys a lot of credit in these last few paragraphs, but remember, it's still me writing this!!

Creative Music Consultants

914-741-0771

DOG YEARS

You recorded your demo. You took your photos and made the video. The band looks and sounds as good as ever. You sent off your promo package to all the clubs and agents in town. Now, all you have to do is sit and wait for the phone to ring.

And wait you will. Remember the phrase, "you can wait until the cows come home"? Well, you're waiting to hear back from club managers and agents. This means the cows will come home and probably have enough time to teach themselves macramé before your phone rings. At least, it will feel like that.

There is a simple reason for this: Your biological clock is ticking. You are living and dying on that phone call. You know if the band doesn't get some work, it will fall apart. You understand the fact that a few members of the band can't pay the rent without a few more gigs. On the other hand, the person booking the club appears to be moving at glacial speed. The booker is operating in "real time." The band is aging in dog years. It's a 7 to 1 ratio. You hoped that you would hear something by tomorrow. You'll be lucky to hear something a week from tomorrow.

At first glance, this might seem unfair, but you need to see the other side of this business. The person responsible for entertainment at the club-let's call her Mary Ellen Wadsworth II- is fielding packages from several other bands. It's Mary Ellen's job to sift through these packages, hoping to find a few bands that are appropriate for the club. Then, she must check their schedules to find some available dates. Each step may have a lag time of a day or two. On Monday, Mary Ellen calls band # 1 with a few dates. The members of Band # 1 all get together and discuss their availability. Do they want to work on the drummer's birthday? Does the statute of limitations expire on that "thing" with the singer? It could take a few days before Band # 1 responds.

Poor Mary Ellen. In many small clubs and restaurants, the resident Mary Ellen has other responsibilities. She might be the bartender or day manager in addition to booking the entertainment. She is doing her darnedest to keep things organized, but it's a hard job. Meanwhile, you have called her 4 times this week. So have all the other bands. You've gotten no response. It's no fun for anyone. It's been months and she still hasn't booked your band. There is only one way to avoid all this. You must sleep with Mary Ellen.

BOTTOM LINE:

Booking gigs might very well be the hardest part of being a musician. You can't get a gig without doing a good audition or recording a proper demo. It is essential to have a good, tight band to do the audition or the demo, but doing gigs is the only way to get a band good and tight. It's an awful situation.

You need to find a way to either convince a band to hang together long enough to get the gig or convince a club to hire you immediately. I'm not really condoning sleeping with Mary Ellen in order to get the gig, but you might consider just making out with her in order to get the audition.

And as always, tip your waitress.

DEAR DIARY # 2

Oct. 30, 2005

The gig last night was at a fantastic little restaurant in Ventura, Ca. They hosted a Halloween party. The band was asked to wear costumes. This always presents a bit of a challenge for me. First of all, I hate wearing costumes. Am I the October equivalent of Ebeneezer Scrooge? Not really.

I'm not against the festivities, mind you. I love parties. I adore candy corn. It's just that it can be difficult playing a gig in costume. It's hard to sing while wearing a mask. Accessories such as capes and gloves make it hard to play an instrument.

I never want to take the easy way out and just throw something together for a costume. You know that guy. There's one at every party. The guy that wraps a towel on his head and says he's a New York City cab driver. The girl that shows up in a bra and panties and calls herself a stripper. I hate that!! I strive to do better. I want to express my creativity. I want to be part of the celebration. I want to represent.

Last year, I considered taking the cerebral approach to the costume. No devils, policemen or super heroes for me. I had planned to attend a party dressed as the Magna Carte. How could you beat that? I would most assuredly be one of the select few to be dressed as the famed document signed by King John of England in 1215. Sadly, I found that parchment tears easily. It's also impossible to dry clean. In a crowded restaurant on a holiday weekend, I would probably end up looking like a used cocktail napkin with my ass hanging out. I decided to stay home.

Keeping all this in mind, I split the difference. This year, I wore a White Sox uniform. It made sense. The Sox had just won the World Series. I was topical, for sure. The outfit didn't restrict my playing or singing. There were no giant boots or antennae. Damn, I really like giant boots and antennae.

After the first set, a mermaid waddled up to me. "Wow, you look so authentic. You're dressed as an out of shape baseball player, right? That's so creative! I love it when people put a little thought and effort into Halloween." Next year I'll go as a stripper.

AUDITION AND SUBTRACTION

Auditions can be nerve wracking. They are rarely fun for any of the parties involved. Is there a way to do a good audition? Is there any way for a band to hold a good audition? Are these questions to be answered in this book? Of course, but you'll have to read through a few paragraphs of my ranting and raving first.

Auditions are a vital part of a working musician's life. You are either the bandleader in need of a player or a player in need of a band. In short, someone's always auditioning for something. You should be prepared to do a good job in either of the aforementioned situations.

As a young musician, go on as many auditions as you can. Get a feel for them. Familiarize yourself with the drill. There is an art to it.

WHAT TO DO

1. Be prompt.

Here we go again! You can't believe I'm taking your valuable time by repeating this basic info. Hear this loud and clear: If I had a nickel for every time a musician walked in late with the excuse of bad directions, I wouldn't have to write this book to pay off my gambling debts! Damn those Cleveland Browns!!!

Anyway, showing up late is not the way to introduce yourself to your potential band mates. Make it a point to be there 15 minutes early. In the event of a flat tire, call ahead and let them know to expect you soon. Walking in late is bad. Walking in with the lame excuse, "I would have called but I lost your number" is worse. Remember, this guy might very well be paying $30 per hour for a rehearsal studio to hold this audition.

I abhor latecomers but at least they eventually show up. As a bandleader holding auditions, I often took the total number of players slated to show up on any given day and immediately subtracted 30%. If

I received 10 calls for the drum chair, no more than 7 would show up. The excuses were varied and some were incredibly creative. Many players never bothered with an excuse. They just vanished. The math stayed about the same. Schedule 10, subtract 3 and meet 7. I called this audition and subtraction. It's sad but true.

2. Be prepared.

Often, a band will give you a list of songs to prepare. Don't learn 3 out of 5. Learn all 5 songs! If you can't prepare 5 songs ahead of time, then don't bother showing up. As a player, you need to understand what the band requires. They need a player that can sing and play certain parts and styles. They know what they want. They really want you to be great. Nothing would make them happier than for you to blow them away by knowing the tunes. After all, that's why you're there.

3. Don't whine.

Get used to walking into a rehearsal studio, plugging in and getting to work. The band needs to see 4 guitarists and 3 drummers in a 3 hour slot. Everyone is acutely aware of the fact that you are using rented gear. It's not your amp, it's a house drum kit, blah blah, blah. Stop bitching about it. Stop talking and start playing. Understand that this is the best they can do. At this point, realize that you are being judged as much by your attitude as by your talent.

4. Dress the part.

You will often be judged by your appearance in an audition setting. Don't be insulted. Be versatile. Be open to change. Take a step in the right direction when dressing for an audition. Try to look like the rest of the band.

For instance, a band puts an ad in the local music paper stating auditions are being held for lead guitarists for a young, edgy, aggressive punk band. Do you want to come straight from your day job as a medical supplies sales rep to audition for this band? Do you want them to see you for the first time in a suit and tie? Of course not! The band needs to see your neck to waist, 4 color tattoo of the Ramones at CBGBs. You owe it to yourself to do the right thing. Pull your car behind the diner and change clothes in the back seat.

There are some very successful club bands that play 70's disco. The members wear Afro wigs, bell bottom pants and silk shirts. There are "tribute bands" that take the time and effort to dress exactly like the bands they admire. These bands may not ask you to show up at the audition dressed that way, but they might have some costumes for you to try on when you get there. If so, don't make it look like an imposition. The costume is a job requirement.

BOTTOM LINE:

Be prompt, be prepared, don't whine and dress the part. Follow these rules without question. That way, when you don't get the gig, you'll know it's because you suck. Hey, I told you a long time ago, not everyone is cut out for this type of work.

TRIANGLE
AUDITIONS

4pm

I guess I should have
been more specific

MUSICIAN'S CONTACT SERVICE

I came to Los Angeles on September 13, of 1990. I rented an apartment in Hollywood, as is required for any newly relocated musician. Your second apartment can be by the beach. You can even get a house in the Valley after a few years, but your baptism of fire has to be the Hollywood apartment.

I had no prospects for gigs. I had no auditions set up. I didn't even know how to get an audition. It's a weird feeling to be living in the Mecca of the entertainment business without a gig. I was within walking distance of several major record companies. World famous clubs and theaters were right down the street. I watched limo after limo whooshing rockstar after rockstar down Sunset Blvd. I was surrounded by success but none of it was mine.

On September 14, I saw a sign on the second floor of a strip mall that read MUSICIAN'S CONTACT SERVICE. I didn't know anything about the company but the name was pretty self explanatory. I walked in and filled out a basic information form. Sterling, the owner, was straight forward and helpful, explaining that for a fee, he placed players with bands. It sounded like a good idea. I paid Sterling his fee, shook hands and walked back home.

Within 2 hours, I got a call from a band needing a singing bassist. I agreed to an audition on the following night, even though my musical gear had not yet arrived in LA. This is when I had to rent an amp to do the audition. (see the chapter NY VS. LA) I apparently wowed them at the audition and got the gig. A few weeks later, MCS hooked me up with a trio that played all 60's music. We worked every almost weekend the following year.

I checked in by phone to MCS on a daily basis. I got several demo recording gigs, a ton of sub gigs and a few long term situations. I answered one ad for an acoustic duo that worked Saturday and Sunday afternoons. I kept that gig for 10 years. Another MCS contact took me to Japan for 3 weeks, which is one of the greatest experiences of my life.

I have gotten a tremendous amount of work from MCS over these last 19 years. I am still a proud member today. Every day, I log into the MCS website and see which bands are looking for a singer/bassist/guitarist. The site might have a listing that says, "Acoustic trio looking for a singer/bassist who can double on guitar. Must be very familiar with Beatles and James Taylor." That, of course, is my dream gig. I've actually gotten several gigs from ads just like that one. If I see something interesting, I call or email the band directly. My player profile is listed on the site. With any luck at all, there's a band out there that is looking for a bitter, old, bassist/author to do a steady Thursday afternoon gig at a topless bar 10 minutes from my house. Ring, damned phone. Ring!

BOTTOM LINE:

The Musician's Contact Service is located in the Los Angeles area, but serves the entire country, sometimes listing overseas opportunities. I cannot say enough about my experience with them. There is no wasted time or energy thumbing through local music papers or scrolling through online ads. The player profile answers the basic questions. The work for hire ad describes the band's musical style, number of gigs per month and approximate pay. In essence, you don't get a lot of calls for gigs you don't want and the band doesn't have to audition a lot of players who aren't right for the situation. Musicians are put in direct contact with each other, eliminating any middle men. It got me an audition within 36 hours of and a gig within 80 hours of signing up. I have traveled around the country and the world directly or indirectly from these relationships.

I cited playing the music of the Beatles and James Taylor as my dream gig. MCS has afforded me the opportunity to play with several bands focused on that music. It always seems like such a gift when I am offering exactly what a band needs and really enjoy what the band plays. When it's a good fit, everyone wins and with MCS, it's a good fit a lot of the time.

Contact MCS at Musicianscontact.com

THE SPIRIT OF RADIO

The radio is a musician's best friend. No matter how extensive and current your CD/mp4 collection, the best way to find out what music the public responds to is listen to the radio. Top 40, classic rock, jazz and practically anything else can be found by scanning the dial. This is great for your personal listening pleasure. It can also be a very helpful tool. It gives you an immediate blueprint for what the average listener wants. The station's play list is based largely on audience requests and sales. If the song is selling in the stores and online, it will be on the radio. This holds true for any genre of music.

The radio will give you a very clear idea of what the "average" person is buying and requesting, and that is exactly the audience you want to target. You have already chosen the musical style for your band. You have found the radio stations that play this type of music. You might consider yourself the cutting edge elitist who knows all things musical. Welcome to the club!

Still, your band should appeal to the average listener of this style of music. If you are playing material that is too outside the box, you won't appeal to John Q. Public and he is the one that is paying the bills. You might not have any desire to play the same tired old songs that everyone else plays, but use your head. You had better play enough recognizable tunes to satisfy the audience. Otherwise, you'll be out of work.

If your band is hoping to get classic rock gigs, listen to a classic rock radio station. This list of songs will give your band an excellent place to start. Learn 50 songs that are played often on that radio station and you'll be set for your gig. Satellite radio makes it easier than ever to put together a song list for your band. Simply choose a station that plays the desired type of music. You'll get a great mix of hits and rare, "deep cuts." Deep cuts are the songs that weren't hits, but often have a fan base. A few of these deep cuts can really add some spice to your repertoire, as these are the tunes that make the audience say, "Ah, I haven't heard this song in years. I've never heard a band play this. This band is fantastic! I just wish the bass player would do something with his hair." I hear that a lot.

Taking your musical cues from the radio is a pretty good idea. It will give your band a solid basis on which to start. There will still be plenty of work for you to do. It's up to you put together a song list that gives you a good mix of songs that will not only keep your audience but expand it.

BOTTOM LINE:

It's always fun to read the music magazines and see what new songs are rising on the charts. This information is always helpful in giving you some insight as to what band is becoming popular. It's great to keep your ear to the ground and know what's going on in the music business. The radio is still probably the easiest tool to use. I get in the car and listen. If I turn it up loud enough, I can barely hear my wife. I love the radio.

THE RECORD DEAL

Ha! Gotcha! What we need to look at here is not getting a record deal, but how to deal with keeping records for tax purposes. That means putting together an organized overview of dates, income and expenses in order to properly conduct business and file taxes.

Organization is the natural enemy of most artists. After all, we want to free ourselves of the day to day minutia in order to compose our masterpieces. We can't be shackled by the responsibilities of keeping records and balancing checkbooks. In some cases, the Internal Revenue Service will be more than happy to shackle you if you don't.

I'm not about to give tax advice to anyone. That's serious business and should not be taken lightly. I would like to offer some organizational advice.

Keep an organized calendar. It can be on your computer, Blackberry or my personal fave, the old fashioned month at a glance calendar book. The first obvious move is to enter all your gigs throughout the year. Write down the name of the club and the pay. There's a pretty good chance that you would play the same club several times, maybe monthly or even weekly.

Also, write down the mileage from your home to the club and back. These miles you drive can more than likely be deductions on your tax return. Do the same for rehearsal and recording dates. You will need this info at tax time.

Keeping this information is easier than you might think. Once a week, go over your date book. Make sure to include any last minute gigs or last minute cancellations. At the end of each month, enter the total income and miles driven.

Keep a record of all the gear you buy. This includes small items such as strings and drumsticks. These purchases add up over the course of a year.

If possible, get a credit card solely for these purchases. Some credit card companies such as American Express offer a year- end statement. This statement details all purchases and breaks them down into categories such as travel, entertainment, meals, etc. It will tell you exactly what you spent in the course of a year.

My checkbook used to look like a map of the southern sky. I had stars, red lines and arrows all over the place. My penmanship would drive even the most experienced Egyptologist to drink. It was hard for me to get serious about my records, but it was necessary. As a bandleader, I have to pay the musicians by check in order for all parties to have an accurate record of income. I might use 3 drummers and 4 guitarists in the course of a year, so I need to keep track of how much I paid out and to whom. It took some discipline, but I managed to get a handle on it.

In turn, each of these players have worked for 3 or 4 bandleaders that same year and need to keep track of who paid them and how much. In most cases, each member receives a 1099 form from each bandleader with whom he has worked. As a player, you need to make sure your numbers jive with the 1099 form you receive. You can't assume the bandleader is correct. You must keep your own set of records.

Your total tax picture will include amortization, depreciation and lots of other stuff that nobody understands except your accountant. You should absolutely talk to a tax preparer for all the details. These few tips could really help. The dates, pay and miles can easily be logged in your calendar. Your checkbook will track your payment to other players and help you arrive at the total for the 1099 form you send them. A credit card will track your other expenses, big and small. All of these can be checked daily if needed. Your calendar and checkbook should always be at your fingertips. You can check your credit cards online or with the monthly statement. Get serious about your record keeping. You'll be glad you did.

January 2009   9 GIGS   1 REHEARSAL   232 $900
                                                MILES

SUNDAY	MONDAY	TUESDAY	WEDNESDAY	THURSDAY	FRIDAY	SATURDAY	December 2008
Bob's LITEHOUSE DUKES HOT SPOT SIERRA	50 × 2 = 22 × 1 = 14 × 2 = 20 × 3 = 12 × 1 =	100 22 28 60 12	$900 222 miles +10 232	1 New Year's BOB'S CAFE $100	2	3 $100 THE LITE HOUSE	S M T W F S 1 2 3 4 5 6 7 8 9 10 11 12 13 14 15 16 17 18 19 20 21 22 23 24 25 26 27 28 29 30 31
4	5	6	7	8	9 DUKES $100	10 DUKES $100	January 2009 S M T W F S 1 2 3 4 5 6 7 8 9 10 11 12 13 14 15 16 17 18 19 20 21 22 23 24 25 26 27 28 29 30 31
11	12	13 (REHEARSE) 10 miles	14	15 BOB'S CAFE $100	16	17	February 2009 S M T W F S 1 2 3 4 5 6 7 8 9 10 11 12 13 14 15 16 17 18 19 20 21 22 23 24 25 26 27 28
18	19 Martin Luther King Jr. Day (US)	20	21	22 100 THE HOT SPOT	23 100 THE HOT SPOT	24 $100 THE HOT SPOT	March 2009 S M T W F S 1 2 3 4 5 6 7 8 9 10 11 12 13 14 15 16 17 18 19 20 21 22 23 24 25 26 27 28 29 30 31
25	26 Lunar New Year	27	28	29	30	31 SIERRA BAR $100	April 2009 S M T W F S 1 2 3 4 5 6 7 8 9 10 11 12 13 14 15 16 17 18 19 20 21 22 23 24 25 26 27 28 29 30 May 2009 S M T W F S 1 2 3 4 5 6 7 8 9 10 11 12 13 14 15 16 17 18 19 20 21 22 23 24 25 26 27 28 29 30 31 Office DEPOT

In the calendar above, your nine $100 gigs are listed with the round trip miles. You might want to put more info such as start times, band names, etc. on the same page. That's fine. For the moment, we'll just list the miles and the income for your acoustic twosome, Duo-Nucleosis.

Bob's Café is 25 miles each way, 50 miles round trip. You played at Bob's twice this month for a total of 100 miles driven. The rehearsal date is circled and I would like to bring it to your attention. Are miles driven to a rehearsal studio a valid expense? The answer is yes. Add those miles (you fill in the number) to the total. Also, remember to include the rehearsal studio rental as a deduction.

Below, we'll list some expenses for your wedding band, Damn The Tuxedos. Keep in mind, this is a list that you will submit to your accountant. He will decide which expenses are legitimate.

Musical expenses for Damn The Tuxedos 2009

Warrior 5 string bass.............................$2100

Bass case..$65.99

Strings (6 sets, $22 per).........................$132.00

2x10 bass cab repair.............................$165.00

Bass amp rental (replacement during repair)...$120.00

Monthly rehearsal studio rental ($50 per x 12) $600.00

Mileage (business only)..................................12,000

Next is a checkbook for your 4 piece rock band, The Butter Knives.

Each player's name is followed by a one letter code to denote the instrument. "K" for keyboards, "B" for bass and "G" for guitar. It helps me remember some of the substitute players whom I haven't had the chance to work with often. Check out the musicians list at the back of the book. I've worked with over 200 players, so I'll take all the help I can get remembering who did what and when.

NUMBER	DATE	TRANSACTION DESCRIPTION	PAYMENT/DEBIT (-)	CODE	FEE (-)	DEPOSIT/CREDIT (+)	$		
117	4-1	DAVE WILLIAMS (G)	100						
118	4-1	Bob TURNER (B)	100						
119	4-1	J. ROSS (K)	25						
120	4-1	K. PUTNEY (D)	100						
121	4-8	R. JEFFREY (K)	100						
122	4-8	DAVE WILLIAMS (G)	100						
123	4-8	Bob TURNER (B)	100						
124	4-8	STEVE OTTO (D)	100						

To reorder call 1.800.652.1111. Thank you for banking with Bank of America

You can see that on the gig on April 1, the keyboardist J. Ross was only paid $25. This is not an April Fool's joke. J. Ross owes me considerable money for playing bass on his last record, so I'm withholding some of his pay. Don't screw with me, piano boy!

There are some different names on the 4/8 date because subs were needed.

My one letter code system comes into play here. When preparing my taxes 8 months later, you might need to be reminded who you hired and what instrument he played. I might have hired a second keyboard player for a cocktail hour so I'll have 2 "K's" in my checkbook for that date and I'll know it's not a mistake. Of course, my single letter code has some serious flaws. Does "T" stand for tuba, tambourine or trombone? Are you sure that "xylophone" doesn't start with a "Z"? You might want to develop a more sophisticated system. Maybe you don't need it at all. Maybe you can memorize all your players. If your memory is that good, you probably remember how to spell xylophone. You'll do just fine.

BOTTOM LINE:

The business of music can be overwhelming at times. Checks, deposits, deductions, expenses and mileage can be a lot to handle. In the examples in these last few pages, we have a calendar page, an expense list and a checkbook register. These 3 tools cover a lot of ground. You have to keep up with each of these tools, which in turn will help you manage the 3 other tools in your band. OK, that was cheap, but you had to see it coming!

Keeping your calendar and checkbook up to date is a necessity. Keep as many receipts for purchases as possible, as the physical receipts will be needed in addition to the list of purchases and credit card year end summaries. Again, check with your tax preparer for more advice on these matters.

CASINO ROYALE

Casinos seem to be popping up everywhere. In the 60's, they were only in Las Vegas and Reno. In the 70's, they opened in Atlantic City. Now, there are hundreds across the US and Canada. These casinos open up a great deal of opportunity for musicians. Most casinos have a lounge. These lounges are a terrific source of work for a solo pianist, an acoustic duo or a 4 or 5 piece band. These lounge acts usually do 4 sets per night. Often, a showroom is also in the casino, where the bigger show bands perform a 90 minute show in a concert setting. These two venues in one building give the average musician a lot of chances to suck.

These lounge gigs can be lucrative. The pay is usually better than a local club. It's usually a multi-nighter. There are thousands of potential fans and clients everyday. You can hand out a lot of business cards in 4 hours in this environment. Be aware that each house has its own policy on selling merchandise. Check with the boss before trying to sell your CDs to casino patrons.

The house provides a PA, lights and sound man. You have a real stage constructed for a band, as opposed to the corner table that has to be moved in your favorite restaurant to make a "stage." The band is often required to dress a little sharper in order to be on these casino stages. The show looks, feels and sounds more polished than the casual pub gig.

The lounge is where patrons stop in for a drink, a bite to eat and a chance to stop losing their rent money for a few minutes. Couples come in to dance for a while. Others sit at the bar and play the electronic poker machines while listening to the band. Guys stand in the back and try unsuccessfully to hit on the waitresses. Watching those poor guys from the stage is so entertaining for me! Who has fielded more pick up lines than a cocktail waitress in a 24 hour casino? She smiles sweetly and you give her a wink with your generous tip. You've ordered 7 glasses of OJ just to hang around. You actually asked, "So, where you from?" You've been shot down 3 times already and you don't even know it. C'mon, fellas. You have a better chance of winning that candy apple red Corvette at the nickel slots. I really enjoy the show, though.

These casino lounges often book some the best club bands in the area. I have always enjoyed playing the casino lounge circuit. On rare occasions, I have also really enjoyed being a spectator. There was always a responsive crowd. After all, many of these people are on vacation. There are hundreds of tourists in these casinos. Everyone is there to have fun. Nobody looks at the time in these places, so a late night crowd is the norm. The band, the atmosphere and the audience are all geared for a party every night.

The showroom is a much different vibe than the lounge. These "A" rooms seat 400-3000 people. The headliners that perform there have a proven track record and often a few hit songs to their credit. The performers range from up and coming acts to well established names. These acts attract a much different audience than the lounge bands. The showroom audience is made up largely of fans of the act. These fans are not just passers-by. They waited patiently online to see the act in a concert setting. No one is coming and going. Everyone arrives early and stays to the very end of the show. The audience is seated for the entire 90 minutes. This puts much more focus on the performers, as there are no distractions such as the TVs and video poker games in the lounge. There are still those guys in the back hitting on the waitresses. Man, they are relentless!

These concert stages are fantastic. Many of the casinos have state of the art sound and lights. The stage is huge. The monitoring is perfect. The backline is often top shelf, with several options on any given piece of gear. I am always presented with at least 2 choices of bass amps and 3 vocal microphones. The musicians can't help but feel a sense of accomplishment when performing in these A rooms. I always feel that my thousands of bar gigs are paying off when I get an opportunity to perform on these stages. It also gives me something to talk about at the bar gig I wind up doing the next day. 2 of my favorite casino show rooms are Fallsview Casino in Niagara Falls and Casino Rama about an hour north of Toronto. I don't know what it is about that part of Canada, but they sure know how to put together a first class showroom. Maybe it's the water. Probably the beer.

MEET AND GREET: THE ART OF MEETING AND GREETING PEOPLE YOU WOULD RATHER NEVER HAVE TO MEET OR GREET AGAIN
OR
HOW TO SMILE AT COMPLETE STRANGERS FOR A LONG TIME
OR
HOW TO SAY "THANK YOU FOR COMING TO THE SHOW MRS. WILLOUGHBY" WHEN YOU REALLY WANT TO SAY, "DIE, BITCH, DIE!!!"

Before or after an A room show, the artists often do what is called a "meet and greet." A meeting room is set aside for the entertainers to shake hands and sign autographs. (The band is generally referred to as "the talent." The stars of the show are referred to as "the artists.") It's a great opportunity for the general public to meet their musical heroes and a chance for the artist to meet the folks that made his career possible.

I have played with many established acts from the British Invasion of the mid 60's. Peter and Gordon and Gerry and the Pacemakers both have incredibly loyal fan bases. They are mostly older folks, but with boat loads of enthusiasm. They clap and sing along. They sometimes dance in the aisles, resulting in a unique convergence of DIRTY DANCING and COCCOON. (Hey, I'm allowed to make jokes like that! I'm officially old at 51). When these fans get a chance to meet the artists, it is always interesting for everyone involved.

The meet and greet always unearths a few stories. Fans arrive with vintage vinyl records from the 60's and 70's to be signed. "Hey, I met my wife at one of your concerts in Ontario in 86." I never knew if he was thanking us or blaming us. Many folks arrange their family vacations around our schedule and come to see us every year. One group of women called the Godiva Girls travels all over the country to attend every one of our Peter and Gordon shows. These women are far and away the best fans in the world. We have all become friends. We often make time to grab a cup of coffee with them before the show or a drink after the show. I am always amazed to see them show up in so many different cities. We're always a little sad on those rare occasions when one or two of the girls can't make it to the show.

Sometimes, it can seem a little crazy. Fans travel all over to see a band for the 100th time, waiting on line to buy the tickets for the show and then waiting on another line just to get a hand shake and an autograph. It's at these times that you realize the power of music. Whether it was the song that was playing on the radio during your first kiss or the song you chose for your first dance as man and wife, music has played a major part in most everyone's life. The audience relates to these songs and to the entertainers who perform them. The meet and greet is the perfect way for John Q. Public to meet the people responsible for such meaningful music.

John Q. Public can be a dopey bastard! JQP, as he is known, sometimes refuses to wait behind the velvet rope. JQP doesn't always understand that the artist he wants to meet has been on 5 planes and 6 vans in the last 4 days and can't wait to get 3 hours sleep before doing it all over again. John Q can't believe you don't remember him. "Norfolk, Virginia. 1997. I was the guy in the gray jacket. I told you I was your biggest fan and you autographed my sister. Then, I waived to you from the glass elevator in the hotel. C'mon, you must remember me. I was the one who yelled, "You guys rock!"

These meet and greet sessions are flattering but exhausting. There is an unending stream of idle chatter, which in a very short while starts to sound less like words and more like someone dropped a box of silverware down a flight of steps. It's a cacophony of blah blah that is so crushingly mundane as to make the Pope himself question the existence of Divinity, for, if there is a God, why he doesn't smite these people in great Biblical fashion, or, at the very least, send them all to the buffet.

For many artists, the meet and greet can be a mind numbing experience. Most fans are gracious and thoughtful. Some are clinically goofy. I don't know how the artists deal with it. I may never know because nobody lines up to see me. I'm not the artist, I'm just the fat, middle aged bassist. I get questions like, "Is that a bass or a guitar?" "How long have you been left handed?" "Why do you look so much thinner on stage?" That's OK. I get to jump ahead of them at the buffet.

BOTTOM LINE:

I can only hope that every band will have the kind of support that we have received from fans. Our Godiva Girls are very special, indeed.

MULTIPLE CHOICE

This test is not designed to challenge or enlighten you. It's just a result of me having too much caffeine in my system. For best results, take this multiple choice test at 4 AM. These results will be best for me, not you. At 4 AM, there's a much better chance this will be funny.

1. Your drummer is great but your bassist is awful. You should

    a. fire the bassist.
    b. suggest your bassist take some lessons.
    c. keep the bassist in the band because he's a loyal friend.
    d. get a lousy drummer, pay the rhythm section less and you keep the difference.

ANSWER: D-nobody cares how you sound. Take the money.

2. A club offers you steady Wednesdays, but for low pay. You should

    a. take the gig because the band needs to get tight.
    b. tell the owner to screw himself for insulting you with that amount of money.
    c. take the gig, show up late, play too loud, leave early and steal all the dinner rolls.
    d. try to negotiate a reasonable deal for more money based on bringing a lot of people and develop a following.

ANSWER: A-not that C is the wrong answer, but you'll do that on every gig anyway.

3. The city ordinance requires your band to stop playing at 1 AM, but hot girls are still dancing to your music at 1:05. Do you keep playing?

    a. Yes.
    b. Yes, definitely.
    c. Oh, Hell yes.

d. Yeah.

ANSWER: Didn't you hear me? I said hot girls are dancing!!

4. You are about to dump your girlfriend when, at her hormonal apex, she suddenly offers to buy you a vintage Strat if you'll stay with her. You should

    a. dump her.
    b. stay just for the Strat.
    c. tell her to throw in a Marshall stack and you'll think about it.
    d. tell her you love her and while she's out buying the guitar, bang her room mate.

ANSWER: B-do the moral thing and just stay for the Strat.

5. Your accountant asks you to explain some expenses. You should

    a. look puzzled.
    b. explain that you didn't know you had to pay taxes.
    c. explain that you didn't know you had an accountant.
    d. tell him that if he makes this go away, you won't report him for sexual advances.

ANSWER: A-look puzzled. It will come so naturally.

6. Your barber shop quartet...OK, I can't even finish this one!!

7. You are in the worst band in town playing in the worst club in town. Ned, your day job supervisor at CRAP-MART tells you he's tired of you arriving late every morning after a gig. You immediately

    a. quit the band and become a loyal employee of CRAP-MART.
    b. quit your day job and pursue your dream.
    c. become more responsible and do both jobs more

efficiently.

  d. offer the boss a backstage pass to your next show.

This one deserves a little explanation. Here goes.

It can't be A because CRAP-MART doesn't really have what anyone would call a "loyal employee." They have zombies with name tags.

It can't be B because one look at your life tells me you've lost the capacity to dream.

Do I really have to explain why C is not the answer?

ANSWER: D-If Ned has been working at CRAP-MART long enough to become supervisor, he's very likely to be lonely, desperate, self deprecating and depleted of several essential vitamins and nutrients. A free ticket to hear your sorry ass band in that deathtrap of a club will undoubtedly be the best thing that's happened to him since the FISHING CHANNEL.

8. Bass strings cost $25, but you only have $20. The question is how did a bassist ever get 20 bucks?

  a. He received it in a birthday card from his Grandma.
  b. He borrowed it from his girlfriend.
  c. He received it in a birthday card from his girlfriend's Grandma.
  d. You got me. I'm all out of ideas.

ANSWER: B-but we might say "stole."

9. A fan sends 4 beers to the stage while the drummer is taking a solo. You quickly

  a. put one beer aside for the drummer so he can have a refreshing beverage after his solo.
  b. tilt your head back and pour both beers down your throat

simultaneously. Then, give the drummer the finger.

   c. hide the beers and deny ever seeing them. Hide them under the set list. He never looks at that.

   d. hand the drummer the beer and say, "That'll be $3.50."

ANSWER-Ok, I really hate to answer a question with a question, but how good a friend is this drummer? The answer is D. Screw him. He's a drummer.

10. You are on your way to a gig. You get lost because

   a. you so rarely get a gig.

   b. you're so stupid.

   c. you wrote the directions on a Twinkie and then ate it.

   d. you can't remember if you should have made a right as soon as you left your house or made a left right after you locked the door.

ANSWER- all of the above. You must have seen that coming.

10a. While lost, you ask the homeless guy wiping your windshield for help with the directions. You call this guy

   a. buddy

   b. chief

   c. sir

   d. dude

ANSWER B-but only for the benefit of the curious on-lookers. When you call him Chief, he'll have a flashback from the Falklands War and detain you in a military style choke hold. This will be wildly entertaining for the folks watching from the nearby bus stop.

10b. as you regain consciousness, you realize that this homeless guy is singing while he's rummaging through your wallet and he has a far better voice than your vocalist. He also knows the words. You have no choice but to

a. hire him on the spot, drive him to the gig and make your ex- singer finish washing your windshield.
b. Tell all your friends that he's Jim Morrison. Then, you'll both get laid.
c. Showcase his stench, announcing to the audience that this is the smell of pure rock and roll.
d. Make him fight the ex-singer and put the video on YOUTUBE.

"All of the above" for 2 questions in the same test would show a lack of creativity on my part. Let's just say any 3 of the 4 choices will work.

PASSION PLAY

Let's assume that you have a burning desire to perform, entertain, write and record. Music is your life. It is all you ever want to do. It sounds as though music is your passion.

I know it is for me. Every aspect of music is exciting to me. I have been playing music for 30 years and it's still the only thing I want to do. I love singing and playing to a live audience. I love the challenge of getting onstage or in the studio with new musicians. I love the process of writing a song by starting with random scribbles in a notebook.

Driving to a gig is always a little more fun than driving to a day job. Getting on a plane to go do a show still makes me giggle. The thought that someone has asked me to fly across the country to hear me play music is almost unbelievable. I feel honored.

This passion for music is the driving force in my life. It is this passion that has allowed me the luxury of doing what I want to do for a living. A musician's life certainly has its ups and downs, but I wouldn't trade it for the world. I can honestly say I have no regrets.

If you are able to do what you love for a living, it's hard to have too many regrets. If you can manage to do so for a few years, you should count your blessings. If you can still make a living after 30 years, as is my case, then you have very little about which to complain. Of course, musicians complain all the time. As goes the old joke, "how do you get a musician to complain?" "Give him a gig." This tired old joke has a lot of truth to it. I've seen it verified a thousand times.

It's obvious to me that my passion for music is as strong today as it was 30 years ago. I don't always see the passion for the music in other players. Of course, these players might disagree with me, but that's because they're idiots. Who else would risk disagreeing with me? They would insist they have passion for the music. I say they are there for the money, the girls or just to get out of the house.

Here are a few scenarios:

A four piece band is playing classic rock at the local pub. Three members of the band are playing and singing their hearts out. They love the crowd and the crowd loves them. One member of the band is looking at his watch. He is more concerned with taking a break. You tell me who is playing with passion.

A singer/songwriter has just finished playing an original set. His manager tells him his performance was way over the top. He wasn't singing, he was screaming. His guitar was out of tune because he played so hard. He gave a 2 minute verbal intro to every song, detailing his inspiration for the lyric. He was attempting to "work the room" by running around the stage. These antics threw off his rhythm guitar playing. He also missed the first vocal line of the chorus because he was busy posing and couldn't get back to the microphone in time. The manager criticized his lack of focus. The singer insists he was just "passionate."

Screaming, jumping and sweating don't always add up to a passionate performance. Trying too hard is acting. It's fake. Most crowds are too smart for that. Never underestimate your audience. A passionate performance is one in which you give your all. That includes having respect for the audience and the music. The song should come first. Play it the way it's supposed to be played. This is true of the solo violinist as well as the heavy metal band.

BOTTOM LINE:

Passion isn't measured in decibels or stage dives. The material should never suffer because the players are showing off. The music should never suffer.

End of discussion.

FANTABULOUS

I know fantabulous isn't a real word. I also know that sometimes "real" words aren't enough to describe the feeling of a truly great gig. "Great" certainly isn't enough. I'm talking about those rare moments when terms like "harmonic convergence" apply.

My first real band (you know, the kind that actually gets paid for gigs) was called FOXFIRE. We were a soft rock trio in New York. I was 19. We played Beatles, Crosby, Stills and Nash, Jackson Browne, etc. We played local clubs and restaurants and loved every minute of it. One particular night, we played a gig in the campus pub at Marymount College in Tarrytown, NY.

The room was small. The stage was small. The pay was low. There was only one item in the plus column: It was an all girl college. It seemed too good to be true. Here were 3 young male musicians in a school of 400 young girls who were living away from home and discovering the effects of beer. The mathematical possibilities seemed endless.

We owned the place from the first note. We played for 4 hours. The girls screamed for 3 encores. They danced on tables and stood on chairs and applauded. After the last song, the Resident Administrator came and thanked us for the greatest show they had seen on that stage. I will never forget that feeling.

There appeared to be a sort of dual reality or parallel universe attached to that room. It held about 60 people. Yet, in my mind's eye, on that one very special night, there were at least 150 screaming girls in a huge hall. We were stars and they were our loyal fans. They couldn't get enough of us and we could have played another 4 hours.

I played the same room several times again with several different bands over the next few years. Some shows were great, but none approached that first one. On some of those later gigs in that room, I tried to rationalize this distortion of reality. "OK, the pub only seats 60. It seems unlikely that 150 could fit. Maybe there were 90 girls and many were standing in the back. Maybe they used to have bigger tables. Yeah. I guess that could account for why there were more people back then. Maybe, just maybe."

I have since decided that, undoubtedly, there were no less than 150 flawlessly beautiful girls singing every word to every song along with me on that absolutely perfect gig. It's possible that my mind's eye has a touch of myopia, but the feeling I had that night will live forever. There is only one word for it. Fantabulous.

THE NAME GAME

Finding a name for your band can be difficult. You want to project a certain image. You want a catchy name. You'd like something recognizable, but you can't take someone else's name. If your name as it appears on your birth certificate is Elvis Presley, you might be out of luck. You probably can't market yourself as an entertainer or use that name onstage. There are lawyers who would be all too happy to explain why you cannot.

I have often listened to the music of violin virtuoso Itzhak Perlman. Perlman is unrivaled and stands alone at the top of his craft. What if he had a less musical but more athletic cousin, Sweat Sock Perlman? Could Sweat Sock trademark his name as a musical act? I don't know.

I do know this: it's a great name for a band. Or a puppet.

Consider what type of gig your band might be doing when choosing a band name. For instance, The Kingdom of the Damned Jazz Trio might not get a lot of work on the supper club circuit. (Wow! That's another great name. Man, I really have a knack for this. Hey, The Knack…oh, that's been used already).

This name thing can be a pain in the neck. You all have to agree on one name, but everyone has their own concept of what is best. It seems an impossible task. Here is an idea that just might work. Let's say there are 4 members in your band. Each member writes down a list of 5 possible band names. Put the lists together and eliminate the obvious bad ones, i.e. The Strato-Bastards, The La Brea Guitar Pits, The Instru-Mentalists, Shred Flintstone, Little Endorphin Annie. If history is any indication, there should be no less than 15 really bad ones.

That leaves 5 names and 4 votes. If you're rehearsing at the drummer's house, he gets 2 votes. If the guitarist owns the van, he gets 3 votes. If the bass player does the booking, well, it's about time he did something. He gets no votes! The keyboardist doesn't even know you're voting. He's still reading the manual, trying to get that B-3 sound. The winner is the name with the most votes. Case closed. Problem solved, until tomorrow morning, when everyone realizes what a terrible mistake you've made by agreeing to call yourselves "PEGASUS."

BOTTOM LINE:

I really like the name Little Endorphin Annie.

FILM AT 11: MAKING THE VIDEO

A video presentation can be the most effective tool a band or artist can use to get work. Several TV channels such as MTV and VH1are dedicated to videos of major acts, but there are also hundreds of local cable shows, webcasts and webisodes that showcase unsigned bands. There are many types of videos. Some are creative and tell a story. Others are live performance videos. Videos are often fantastic. So is the budget.

Let's assume that your band does not have a lot of money. (That's a safe assumption because that sentence contains the words "band" and "money." The NOT is usually implied.) Very few bands have much disposable income. You need to get the most bang for your buck. Creating a video takes some thought and some work. The artist needs to make some choices before you start shooting the video. Here are a few things to consider.

LIVE VIDEO

A live video is one that records the audio and visual as it happens. Nothing is pre-recorded. The goal here is to capture the energy and power of a live performance. You want to catch the magic that happens when a band plays to an audience. You want to do more than hear the music. You want to feel the music. You want to see the sweat on the singer's brow and watch the drummer's sticks splinter. This is the stuff that can't be choreographed. This is real. This is live. This is it.

In order to achieve this goal, you have to pay attention to the details. The lighting has to be right. The sound has to be right. The camera work must be steady. You need to get good looking shots with a good camera. The sight lines must be correct. You want the audience to be involved without being detrimental to the cause. Is the crowd obstructing the long shots? Are the people so noisy that they interfere with the recording? You need to consider these possibilities before the musicians play a single note.

When the band does play a note, will it be the right one? Let's face it, mistakes happen. They fly by in a live setting. They live forever on DVD.

Some smaller miscues can truly add some character to the show. The solo that went 4 bars longer because the sax player was wailing and the crowd was eating it up was a cool bit of improvisation. The singer sang the last verse twice but the band followed seamlessly. That stuff is pure gold. Other mistakes, however, will haunt you for the rest of your natural life.

PRE-RECORDED

You flap your lips for 4 minutes but nothing comes out.

1. You're a lawyer.

2. You are lip syncing to your new video.

Lip syncing has become an art form. It's the art of making believe you are singing. It is not an afterthought or a possibility. It's a requirement. If you are going to lip sync in a video, you better practice first. It's harder than it looks.

The basic idea is this: You record the music for your video in a recording studio. You basically make a record. You mix and master it. When you are ready to film, you lip sync to the pre-recorded CD. This is an interesting twist. The use of pro tools and pitch correction resulted in this recording on which you were hardly singing in the first place. Now, you're totally and utterly making believe you are singing to a track of you hardly singing. Wow! What has happened to us? I guess that's a whole different book. Anyway, the pre-recorded method gives you more control over the sound of the video. You already know what it will sound like. You can now concentrate on what it will look like.

Naturally, you have many of the same issues of the live video. (Lighting, camera work, wardrobe and the lawyers I insulted will undoubtedly show up with papers for me! Here we go again!!) You now have to add the issue of lip syncing to that list.

Great lip syncing goes unnoticed. Bad lip synching will turn your video into a martial arts film from 1972, only less popular because nobody punched the drummer in the chest and ripped out his beating heart and showed it to the camera. NOTE TO DEATH METAL BANDS: Please do not misconstrue the last example as creative input on my part. The Surgeon General has determined that ripping the drummer's heart out can be hazardous to his health. Leave the drummer alone. As for that damn lawyer, I'll give you $20 if you can even find his heart.

If you are a female singer in a club band, looking and acting like a slut in your video will get you gigs. The club owner will watch half the video with the sound off while firing the daytime bartender and fixing the ice maker. He'll watch you prance around with your pouty lips and your jet black eyeliner and realize he must have you…to perform at his club. You're in.

If you are doing a wedding video, look good, but don't ever look hotter than the bride. You will never get booked. The bride and groom to- be will take a look at the video in hopes of hiring you. The groom will look at your video with one eye, while attempting to watch his prospective wife with the other. The bride has scanned 4 seconds of the video and that's all she needs. Her micro-processing brain has instantly calculated your waist size, cup size and natural hair color. Now, she is watching her man to see if he reacts appropriately.

He knows she's watching him and is ever so careful about his next move. The slightest flinch, the faintest smile, any sign of perspiration even on the molecular level is the "tell" that he finds the chick singer attractive, which is unacceptable. This is more than a poker game. This is more than a gun fight. This is full contact bazooka Texas Hold 'Em. The groom never wins this contest.

There is a lot of pressure on the women in these videos. After all, it's a visual presentation. The 4 ugly guys behind you will usually go unnoticed. In the club video, they'll be the 4 ugly guys in tee shirts. In the wedding video, they'll be the 4 ugly guys in tuxedos. Sometimes they'll be the 3 ugly guys in tuxes because the drummer forgot and only brought a tee shirt. In any event, the girl up front is the centerpiece of the video.

BOTTOM LINE:

Making a video requires a lot of thought and some money. Don't let that deter you. Be smart and creative. You'll get a good product that showcases your band and allows you to keep the only job you ever wanted. You'll be glad you made the investment.

CHURCH GIGS

I had never done a church gig until a few years ago. I'm not a member of a church and didn't know that church gigs existed. My spiritual beliefs are my own and I wasn't sure how I would feel about playing at a church service. I wasn't sure how I would be received, either.

My questions were answered almost instantly at my first service. My good friend, Scott, who was a member of the congregation, had recommended me. I was welcomed, quite literally, with open arms. "Any friend of Scotty's…" was the opening line of everyone I met. The religious denomination of any of the musicians never seemed to be an issue.

The players were great. The tunes were strong. The attitude was professional. The response from the congregation was unbelievable.

All band members were aware that I had never heard the material. I was assured that I was not going to be judged by my mistakes. They were happy to have me and I was happy to be there.

I have been on a thousand gigs where the musicians met for the first time 30 minutes before playing a wedding. This was much different. On the wedding gig, 80% of the songs are standard fare. On the church gig, however, none of these songs had ever been top 40 radio tunes. Some are original compositions by church members. Other tunes might be heard on inspirational radio stations. I was given charts, but I don't read music. (I struggle with the simplest of lead sheets and fake books. I'm much better off just using my ears and watching the guitarist's hands.) I had to be on my toes and my band mates were great at helping me through the gig. It was relaxed and professional and it was a wonderful experience.

I have had the chance to do several of these gigs. The few I have done have been interesting in that many of the services have not been held in traditional church buildings. One service is held weekly in a movie theater. The Church officials had made arrangements to use the theater on Sunday mornings before business hours. From 8 AM to noon it was a house of worship. At 1 PM, the latest summer blockbuster was being shown on the big screen. Across town in Hollywood, a nightclub is used in the same fashion. For 3 hours on Sunday, the room is transformed. Utilizing these spaces is pretty innovative. The service and congregation are the same as that of the standard church. It seems to work out for everyone.

BOTTOM LINE:

The message of fellowship and brotherhood is often at the center of the sermon and I'm always eager to perpetuate those values. These musical performances usually consist of approximately 8 tunes. The service lasts about 60 minutes. The band arrives 45 minutes prior to the service for a quick rehearsal. The pay is usually $100. That's not bad for a musical challenge, a built in audience and a much appreciated dose of spiritual uplifting.

THE MYTH OF DEMOCRACY

I have made 2 really bad choices in my life.

1. I walked barefoot in a public restroom.

2. I tried to be democratic in a band.

I know nothing of real politics. I know a lot about band politics. Democracy doesn't work in a band situation. Dictatorship works very well, thank goodness. After doing a little research, it appears that the word "democracy" is a bit vague and has several meanings and interpretations. The word is often misused, adding to the confusion. It stems from the Greek demokratia, which means "rule by the people." Democracy is often used to depict a situation where all have a voice and the situation is fair and equal, and free elections are held in order to choose representatives. This is the widely used interpretation and the one that we will take issue with here.

All bands start out on the same path. Everyone has an equal say. Everyone does equal work. Each member contributes equal money to get the band up and running. It all seems quite natural and easygoing. That will not last. Things will change. They have to change.

All of this equal nonsense will end soon because you will all realize that there is no such thing as "equal." Put away your calculators and get some real world education here. I would like to cite some examples of this type of democracy failing.

All 4 members of the band are required to rehearse every Thursday night at 7. The bass player works in a warehouse that doesn't close until 7. If he has to leave early and lose an hour's wage in order to get to rehearsal, he's not seeing this situation as equal.

Each member owns an equal share of the PA, but only the drummer has a van that can carry the PA. Sure, the rest of the band can help him load and unload at the gig, but the poor drummer has to unload it all by himself when he gets it back to his house.

Now, the 4 musicians can try to rectify these problems by taking on other responsibilities in order to balance things out. The fix is temporary. Everyone has their own value system. Spending an extra 50 bucks is nothing to the guy with the good paying day job, but way too much for the guitarist trying to eke out the rent. The extra hour at rehearsal is a lot to ask from the singer with a wife with 2 kids waiting at home. Equal does not exist.

As these scenarios arise, there will undoubtedly be a rift among players. One guy will feel put upon because he has to do all the business of booking gigs and rehearsals. Another feels left out because he isn't involved in the band business. Envy, jealousy and resentment permeate every fiber of your being due to being overburdened and underappreciated.

These feelings are incredibly destructive to a band. They take up all the energy you should be spending on creativity, writing songs, taking lessons, and learning parts. All these negative feelings destroy the band that started out as equal partners in a democratic organization. How can this be avoided? How does a band make it all work?

A bandleader is the answer. How do you decide who leads the band? Natural selection, to borrow a term from Darwin. A leader is usually easy to spot. He's the guy who sees the big picture. Sometimes, he's the one who owns the PA and books the gigs. Maybe he's the lead singer and songwriter. There are people that are just good at directing a band and want to do so. He's the one that gets things done. You don't really elect him. He is the natural leader. He has emerged from the primordial soup and evolved into the band leader that will keep your band thriving while those around you become extinct. Under his direction, you will be the fittest and you will survive.

This in no way, shape or form means the band leader is the smartest person in the band. Again, I remind you that the band leader is a musician, so let's not bandy about the word "smart" with any frequency. However, the word "stupid" can be used with tremendous regularity when discussing musicians.

AUTHOR:

My old band leader was so stupid.

READERS:

How stupid was he?

AUTHOR:

My band leader was so stupid that when I wanted to leave rehearsal early, I would simply throw a towel over his head and tell him it was night. It worked like a charm. It cured his insomnia and I never missed an episode of MURDER SHE WROTE.

Thank you. You've been a lovely audience. Now, back to the book.

The bandleader should be a "can do" guy, but shouldn't have to do everything. He does the bulk of the business, talking to the booking agents and club owners. He organizes rehearsals and books the photo shoots. Some of the other tasks such as mailing lists and cartage are delegated to the other members. This should not be insulting to the other musicians. This is merely assuming a role in the organization. Everyone "might" have a voice in the band, but not everybody wants to be involved in the day to day business of the band. One might choose to simply be the good, reliable keyboard player. He's a passionate player committed to his band, but he's not business minded. He doesn't want too much responsibility other than playing and singing. That's not a sin. That's very common. A good bandleader will learn to take all the positive energy from his comrades and delegate accordingly. Each member seeks his own level and the bandleader fills in the cracks. If everyone involved is honest and realistic, the band will thrive without all the drama.

Keep in mind, the bandleader wasn't elected and not everyone has an equal say. It's not always smooth sailing, but it seems to work. It's not a democracy. It's just a band.

BOTTOM LINE:

Bands can often seem similar to marriages. Relationships within a band can become dependent, co-dependent, symbiotic and dysfunctional. They can become your greatest love and greatest heartbreak at the same time. Comparing a band to a marriage might appear to some of you as an overstatement. I know a lot of musicians that have a hard time choosing between attending their wife's office Christmas party and doing a gig for $50. You know you should go with your wife, but even she knows you'd rather be at the Safari Room, playing old Stones tunes with your bros. You love your wife, but...see those dot dot dots? They cause trouble. You see it as choosing between an office party and a gig. Your significant other might feel as if you are choosing your music over your relationship.

Music is a harsh mistress, indeed! (You know, that line sounds so great to me because, in my head, Patrick Stuart from Star Trek just gave it a real over the top thespian reading with that edgy British accent. Man, that Patrick Stuart rocks! Oh, my. I think I'm developing a man crush). The ultimate desire of every musician is to play music. If the spouse of that musician understands and accepts that, it's a fantastic relationship. If the spouse does not accept it, well...dot, dot, dot.

I was going to end this chapter with that last paragraph, but my wife read it and suggested I take a more balanced approach to this issue of comparing marriage and bands. It appears as though I was looking at all the negative aspects of these relationships and none of the positive. After some spirited conversation and a quick re-reading of my own words, I concur.

A band, like a marriage, is always a work in progress. It's a dynamic relationship that takes on a life of its own. I once read that a marriage consists of 3 entities: You, your partner and your relationship. Essentially, you sometimes have to treat your relationship like a third person. You're a great person and so is your partner, yet you have some serious problems and your relationship isn't working. When this happens, you have to take steps to fix things. You have to own your actions and take responsibility for your part in the relationship. You have to keep up your end of the bargain. When it works, it's the greatest feeling in the world.

This applies to a band as well. A band is very much like a marriage in that you have to juggle the wants and needs of all parties involved. You need to choose your battles carefully, opting to compromise or stand and fight on any given issue. You must always keep your eye on the prize. Maybe the term "in sickness and in health" should be written into band contracts. It might make musicians look at the big picture more often. If you are lucky enough to have both a band and a marriage that work, you are clearly doing something right.

Boy, am I whipped or what!!??

POLYGAMY

We've established that a band is often like a marriage, so now it's time to practice polygamy. Practice it as often as possible. Work with as many bands as possible and juggle as many gigs as you can. There is one major twist to this practice. You have to be committed to every band.

Yeah. The concept of polygamy is always appealing at first blush, especially to men. All these choices are laid out in front of you like the buffet at Caesar's Palace. You simply pick and choose the one to satisfy you on any particular night. You will enjoy a cornucopia of musical delights (remember, we're talking music) and all is well with your calendar, your wallet and your psyche.

"Conflict" is a word with which you will need to get familiar when practicing polygamy. Conflict will rise up out of the calm and erase your calendar, empty your wallet and twist your psyche like a Coney Island pretzel. There is always some conflict in marriage, thus it stands to reason that there is potential for more conflict in polygamy, because there are more "wives." I am acutely aware of what I just wrote. Hold on, I'll be back in a minute.

Sorry. I just had to grab a pillow and a blanket. I'll make myself comfy on the couch for the next few nights.

Musical polygamy is even more complicated because it involves not just several wives but several bands. You commit to certain dates with certain bands with the best of intentions. Every now and then a conflict arises.

It usually goes something like this:

I am scheduled to play with Bobby and the Toasters one night next month. Today, a band leader called me to offer me 3 nights in Vegas that conflict with the Toasters gig. The Vegas gig pays a lot more and is likely to lead to more work of better pay. The dilemma is obvious. Some people think the choice is to simply play the gig with Bobby and the Toasters because you committed to that one first. Others think the clear choice is to take the better opportunity in Vegas.

I have argued with myself over these conflicts. I have been on both sides so many times that my split personalities are developing split personalities. I try to draw lines such as "at least 2 weeks notice" or "a one hundred dollar difference." I always want to give a band at least a 2 week notice if I have to sub out a gig. I don't usually consider subbing out unless there is at least a $100 difference. Most musicians understand that money is an issue. Still, there will always be those special circumstances that aren't quite so black and white.

The best musicians come with a price. I hire the best guitarist in town for my $200 gig. I have to realize that a higher profile, better paying artist is right around the corner, waiting for my great guitarist. If my guy gets the call, I only ask that he let me know as soon as possible. I wouldn't ask anyone to pass up a great opportunity just to do my club date.

Any musician that wants to trade my gig for a more desirable one is welcome to do so as long as he respects my situation. The more desirable gig doesn't have to be high profile or better paying. If it's a gig you really want and need to do, I would do everything I could to make it happen for you. If you have the chance to play your original music or finally work with that unbelievable sax player who has been calling you for 6 months, I say go for it. Let me know ASAP and I'll do everything I can to make it easy for both of us.

As a player for hire, I have had to make that uncomfortable call to the leader. "I know you have given me a lot of work lately. I really appreciate it. I have a scheduling conflict for next month and I would like to talk to you about it." From that point on, it's my job to make it clear that I am making a request, not a demand. Most of these problems have reasonable solutions. I have asked to sub out a gig, offering to pay for a hotel room for my sub that has a long drive to cover my gig. I have left my bass rig at the club in order to make things easier for the guy filling in. I have returned the favor by subbing for my sub when a similar circumstance arose for him.

Bandleaders and hired guns have to understand that "intent" is the basic tenet of polygamy. It's not my intention to make things difficult for the band if I ask to sub out. It's never my intention as a bandleader to make things hard for the players who want to do another gig. Players and leaders must be willing to compromise in order to make the big picture stay focused. No one needs to be punished. Everyone involved deserves respect. Most of the time, a little patience and a splash of logic makes things right.

Still, there are those "sticky wickets" when there aren't any subs available but the sax player really wants and needs to do the other gig. In those cases, your band is out of luck. These are the tough times that challenge your friendship and business relationship. These are the times when both the player and the leader have to shut up, take a deep breath and go where the universe takes them. These stories don't always have happy endings. Sometimes your gig really suffers because of the missing player. These are the times when you learn what you're all about. Will you hold a grudge? Will you fire your good friend? Hopefully, you won't do either of those. Hopefully, you will both dig deep and realize that you have another million gigs ahead of you. You will forgive, forget and laugh about it from time to time.

SUB OR SUB-PAR?

Using a substitute lead singer is always a scary situation for the band. The sub singer is often a piece of work. Hand the sub bassist or sax player a chart and you're all set. This player will play what is required and very little more. He'll fit right in without sticking out. Hand the sub singer a microphone and find the nearest bomb shelter. He's going to stick out, jump out and give a shout out while letting it all hang out.

Very often, the singer is a type A personality. He walks into the gig wearing sunglasses, no matter what time of day or night. His handshake is firm. He brings his own bottle of water from home. He introduces himself in a confident baritone, super hero voice. "Hello, citizens. I'm Deke Fingersnap. I'm here to help." Before you can ask, he proceeds to recite his entire resume, beginning with his mastering of the glockenspiel at the age of 9. "Yeah, the word prodigy is overused. Let's just say I can throw down on the old g-spiel." Deke then pops his collar, winks at the waitress and tries desperately to convince you that, even at his advanced age, he's in touch with the younger audience. "Kids today are no different. Forget that rap and hip hop stuff. I'll just sing the blues and those beatniks will do the Pony like there's no tomorrow. Am I right or am I right?"

Again, these folks are often type A personalities. They have to be. It's a survival technique. They have to put themselves out there and hope you like them. His job is to first win you over and then win the audience over. Deke is outgoing and straight forward. Chances are he's a pretty good singer. He's probably been doing it for a long time.

Your band should bend but not break in this situation. Deke is now your guy and you have to allow him to do what he does best. Just be sure it's a two- way street. He must allow the band to do what got them the gig in the first place. The sub can never stop the band from doing their show. The band will be different with a sub, but should not be noticeably worse. The band should not be sub-par because of him. You all must make it work. He must fit in. He must learn to lay back and sometimes lay out. Above all else, he must suck in his gut.

The chick sub singer is a little different. Her entrance to your gig usually goes something like this: "Hi, I'm...oh, what was my name again? Dang! Oh, well, it doesn't matter because I'm really hot, but I want to act like one of the guys, so I'll carry my own music stand into the gig. I know one of you guys will fall in love with me by the third set and buy me stuff." She's correct. One of the guys will get her some water. Then, you'll give her your business card, making sure you're the guy she calls when she needs piano lessons. The bassist sees this and vies for her attention by offering to park her car. The drummer counters that move by offering to lease her a car.

She'll probably sing some "unique" harmonies. It's OK. Let her sing anything she wants as long as she's hot. She must be the focus of the band. She must command the attention of the audience. Above all else, she must stick out her chest.

BOTTOM LINE:

Attention young readers!! Doing the Pony is doing a dance from the 60's, not a peep show in Tijuana.

DRUNK AND DISORDERLY

I have had the distinct pleasure of playing music for 30 years with hundreds of players. Many of them were incredible musicians. Most of them were great people. Some were alcoholics. A few were all 3.

Some of my best friends were fantastic alcoholic musicians. There were times that these friends caused me to have some tremendously uplifting musical experiences onstage, only to be followed by some truly horrible events. I won't bother detailing stories of these guys falling asleep onstage, missing rehearsals or driving home at 60 mph on the wrong side of the road. These are tales that we have all heard a thousand times. These are good guys that are suffering from a disease. I shouldn't judge them. After all, they are my friends.

I found myself in a struggle with this dilemma for the better part of my musical life. Am I a bad friend for being mad at them? Do I have the right to be ticked off because one drunken band member got all of us fired from a gig? Am I making it "all about me" if I speak my mind about how their unacceptable behavior makes me feel?

I have asked myself these questions many times in my life. I have spent too much time with band mates that drank too much. Our gigs were always in bars, so I was constantly swimming upstream on this topic. If I asked someone not to drink too much, I was dismissed. "C'mon, Bill, lighten up. One beer isn't gonna kill me." A patron would send a round of drinks to the stage. "Well, we can't insult the guy. Drink up." The term "one for the road" always made me crazy. I would watch in amazement as the singer would climb over a wall of people to get that all important last call drink before getting behind the wheel for the long drive home at 3 AM.

I guess I'm not smart enough to understand the complexities of this addiction. Apparently, I'm not tolerant enough to deal with addicts. I still work for a few alcoholics, but I don't think I'll ever hire one again. I can't deal with the excuses or the nonsense. I shouldn't be expected to pick up someone else's slack or clean up someone else's mess. This is not a lack of compassion on my part. This is the stone cold realization that I am a bandleader, not a counselor or babysitter. The brutal truth is that it's hard to help someone who doesn't help himself. It's hard to be supportive when your friend is drinking himself out of a job. It's even harder to watch your friend drink both of you out of a job.

In my experience, these addicted musicians have put a lot of pressure on me to keep them on the gig. I shouldn't be leaned on to employ someone who isn't capable of doing his job. I never wanted to turn a blind eye to their problem. I tried to talk to them about their problem. If I asked them about their drinking, it was none of my business, but when their job was in jeopardy because of it, I was expected to "understand" and "accept" their situation. I'm sure I'm not the only bandleader who has found themselves in this situation.

These players made it clear to me that they really wanted and needed the gig, not just for the money but for the outlet. We all do it as a creative and emotional release, but some of these friends often said it was even more important to them. Without the music, their drinking would become worse. The pressures of the wife and kids, the mortgage, the job at the office that they hate, would all multiply if they didn't have the band as an outlet. Essentially, the music was the only thing keeping them from going over the edge. This was sometimes mentioned to me by the player himself or by his family member or friend.

I was insulted by many of these discussions. Music was more important to them? The gig was more meaningful to them? They sure didn't act like it. Showing up late, unprepared and drunk doesn't exactly strengthen your position in any work situation. When push came to shove, family members and friends spoke up on their behalf. I often asked if these same people spoke up for me. Did anyone take the alcoholic musician aside and say, "Hey, your buddy Bill is giving you an opportunity to make things right. Your drinking has made his job really difficult, but he's still employing you. Maybe you should straighten yourself out." I don't know if those conversations ever took place.

I have done my share of designated driving. I have made many late night phone calls to make sure that a friend got home safe and sound after a gig.

I tried not to get mad. When I did get mad, I tried to find ways to express my anger without losing control. I was constantly searching for a new way to break through and make this alcoholic realize that he is ruining the band, his personal relationships and probably killing himself. There are 2 ways alcoholics can kill themselves. The slow way is to drink so much for so long that the body breaks down. The quickest way is behind the wheel of a car.

Sadly, I have lost friends in and out of music to both methods.

I'm sure this chapter has caught a few readers by surprise. Is this the same book with the funny little drawings and the goofy stories? Why are we getting all serious all of a sudden? This is not the first time that this book has been a catharsis for me. Writing about these adventures in my life simultaneously brings a flood of treasured memories while dredging up some hard core emotions. My 3 greatest passions are my family, my friends and my music, each of which has been touched by alcoholism. When my best friends, who are in my band, become alcoholics, it's bound to have a dramatic impact on me.

I owe it to you to be honest. I make it clear when I'm joking. I don't think anyone mistakes my dream sequence on page 30 to be factual. I have 'fessed up to being "stooopid." I have worked with many alcoholics and a few drug addicts and it has taken a toll on me. No doubt, it shows in my writing. After 30 years of playing music and 4,200 gigs, I must say I would rather work with sober players.

Many musicians think they play better after a few drinks. Some listeners might disagree. I have heard a few stories about legendary performances by Jimi Hendrix or Janis Joplin while they were drunk or under the influence of something or other. I would respectfully counter those with stories of the thousands of performers on every level that were horrible because of these influences.

I have expressed some tough love here. My involvement in the lives of my alcoholic friends has sometimes been a factor in what eventually got them to help themselves. I did my best to listen to them, employ them and give them the occasional lift home. I also gave them a piece of my mind when I was fed up. I never knew if I was taking the correct approach. I only knew it was honest.

A few years ago, a musician/friend called me to tell me the reason we hadn't spoken in 2 years was because he had gone from drinking to becoming addicted to prescription pain killers. He had recently been let out of jail. He told me how he had been clean for a few months, seen the error of his ways and would never go back to that life again. I found out sometime later that his sobriety didn't last. I haven't heard from him in 7 years.

The following year, a great friend from the past called me out of the blue to tell me that he has been sober for 10 years. He was apologetic about his behavior when we worked together 20 years earlier. He told me that my voice was one of very few that he actually heard in his dark days. He decided to change his life for the better. To this day, he remains sober and healthy. I was so happy to hear about his success that any negative feelings I was harboring completely evaporated. I'm glad I had a positive influence on him. I'm certainly not taking credit for his recovery. That act of strength and bravery belongs solely to him. I never tried to be a counselor or a babysitter. I just tried to be a friend.

If you think you can be a friend to someone with an alcohol or drug problem, contact the following:

Alcoholics Anonymous........www.aa.org

Al-anon.........................1-888-425-2666

MY DRINKING PROBLEM

OK, I thought we could all use a little levity now!! I've misled you. I don't have a drinking problem, not in the traditional sense anyway. As stated in the previous chapter, I have had my share of adventures and mishaps with alcoholics in my bands and in my family. In fact, there are a few generations of alcoholics in my family.

Where is that levity??

I am a pretty clean living guy. I have never had a cigarette, an illegal drug, a joint or a beer in my life. I haven't had a drink since 1979. If I left it at that, one might assume that I was a heavy drinker in 1978. Not so. I think this is a cute little story.

In 1972, my older brother, Steve was at home with a few friends. I was about 13. I asked what he was drinking and Steve said it was a screwdriver. I had a few glasses. It was cool to sit around drinking with my older brother. I never felt ill or drunk. I never did it again. I don't think I ever thought about it again.

Years later, I began working with my band, Foxfire. We would go out to the bars in New Rochelle, NY after rehearsals each week. I was a bit younger than my friends and this was a new scene for me. I simply did as they did. In 1977, that meant I would put on my Dingo boots, order a drink and begin the process of getting rejected by women.

I bellied up to the bar and confidently ordered a screwdriver. The bartender poured it and handed it to me. I took one millionth of a sip and spit it out. I sent it back and was given another. I did this 3 times. I did the same thing for the next few weeks in several establishments. Each drink tasted more horrible than the last. Bartenders changed glasses, bottles of vodka, and squeezed fresh orange juice, all in an attempt to make me happy. None of it worked. Keyboardist Chris said, "Man, Bill drinks a lot of screwdrivers." Guitarist Tom replied, "No, he only orders a lot." It became so silly. I would actually order a drink, take one sip and walk around with it for a half hour, then put it down.

I guess it seemed cooler to be holding a drink than not. It wasn't cool and it certainly wasn't cost effective. I would leave 99% of the drink on the bar.

I went to a Christmas party and actually had a few sips of 2 screwdrivers, by far the most amount of alcohol in my system at any one time. It left a terrible after taste not even Diet Coke could extinguish. I wound up leaving the half glass of soda right next to the unfinished mixed drink.

After a few weeks of this ridiculous ritual, I called Steve to compliment him on being the finest screwdriver maker in the land. "Steve, I have been to every bar in town, but nobody makes drinks as well as you do." His response was focused. "Are you kidding? Are you an idiot? Do you really think I would pour a screwdriver for a 13 year old? Are you an idiot? That was only orange juice. If you had 3 screwdrivers in 20 minutes, you would have passed out. Have you really gone all these years thinking that you had 3 screwdrivers? What are you, some kind of idiot?" From that point on, the words screwdriver and idiot are forever entwined.

About six months later, it was suggested to me that I might enjoy Kailua and cream as a drink. I shared one on 2 occasions, for a grand total of one complete Kailua and cream. I was proud of myself for coming of age and having a drink, until I came to understand the components of the drink. Apparently, I would get homogenized way before I got drunk on that concoction. There was very little booze, but it was a great source of calcium.

On October 12, 1985, brother Steve asked me to be his best man. After making my speech, I toasted the couple with champagne. I was told it was bad luck not to toast, so I dipped my pinky in the drink, said "cheers" and then licked the drop of bubbly off my fingertip.

I repeated that move on April 4, 2000 when my dear friends Peter and Tina had their first child. Whiskey was the drink of choice. It damn near took my head off. Our friend E.B. took sequential photographs, capturing my expressions moving from joy to sorrow as the tiniest hint of alcohol reached my lips. On March 27, 2008, I attended Gordon Waller's wedding in New York City. I once again wet my upper lip with champagne to toast the bride and groom.

That's 3 sips in 23 years. For God's sake, someone cut me off!!

In my life, I have ordered about 20 screwdrivers and 2 Kailua and creams. Or is it Kailuas and cream? You would think I would have gotten a better grasp of the English language before writing a book. The point is that I have ordered many drinks and actually ingested a total of about 5, all in that 16 month span from December of 1977 to March of 1979. This leads me to be very specific about my drinking problem, namely that I can't stand the taste of alcohol, even in the smallest amounts. It really is a problem. I absolutely hate rum cake. I have never had a beer, a smoke or a drug. I haven't had an aspirin in 15 years. But I can't say I have never had a drink.

BOTTOM LINE:

I have spent a lot of time in bars, playing music 4 nights a week for many of my 30 years as a musician. Most people marvel at the fact that I never drank and to this day, this is the topic of conversation on a nightly basis. I am thoroughly enjoying my fame. Many people ask me if I will ever have a real drink. I'd say probably not. After 30 years of $100 gigs, I can't afford to start drinking. It's so expensive. Unless the 99 cent store opens a wine cellar, I think I'll stick to iced tea. Cheers!

OUT OF TUNE IS THE NEW BLACK

Someone said that you know you're getting old when you start sounding like your father. I'm about to age quickly in this chapter. When did it become hip to suck? Really. At what point did it become acceptable to sing and play out of tune?

I really need you to stay with me on this one. I'm not talking about the young band that is just getting their feet wet on the first gig. I'm not talking about a band having an off night. I'm talking about the players that are out there making a lot of money that clearly haven't taken the time to learn their instrument.

I understand the beautiful simplicity of a country song. I can feel the angst and anger of a 3 chord punk song. I get the repetitive groove of a disco tune that packs a dance floor. It's not about the complexity of the music. It's about what the band is trying to say. It's all about the attitude of the players and the passion with which they play the music. I have deep appreciation for all those who play their chosen mode of music with conviction and style.

I still ask the same question: At what point did it become acceptable to sing and play out of tune? When did "out of tune" become "the new black?"

Let's not go round and round on this one. There are folks out there that shouldn't be allowed onstage with an instrument. Period. This isn't politically correct to say, but someone has to say it.

It seems to be getting worse everyday. I used to go to a club and be awestruck by incredible talent. It seems as though there was an endless stream of innovative bands with original sounds. It's not that each player was a prodigy, but they were competent on their instrument and serious about their craft. I am aware of some incredibly gifted players and bands that restore my faith in humanity from time to time. Just not often enough.

In a perfect world, musical expression should be without judgment and without parameters. One should be able to play and sing what moves them. There are no standards to be met, no level of talent or achievement to attain. Yeah, well, in that same perfect world, I'm the power forward for the World Champion New York Knicks and my supermodel girlfriend serves me poached eggs in bed every morning. However, here in Regularville, there are some standards to meet. Sometimes, not enough standards.

ARE YOU FRIGGIN' KIDDIN ME?

We have come to a point where we watch a concert more than listen to it. Performers no longer try to hide the fact that they are not playing and singing. We hear a 20 voice choir and a 40 piece string section coming from 3 guys on stage. Sometimes, those 3 guys are playing instruments in addition to the backing tracks. Sometimes, they're not. What the Hell? How did this happen?

In the 30's and 40's, big band music was popular. It was common for a 10 piece band to play behind a singer. As rock n roll became mainstream, bands became leaner. There were 4 Beatles. Buddy Holly had 2 Crickets with him.

Band members became more identifiable, as each had a musical signature, a sonic fingerprint. The sound of rock n' roll was organic and raw. The palette was limited to mostly bass, drums, keyboards and guitars behind the vocals. These bands had a sound that was very often defined by their limitations.

Many of these limitations were overcome with the advent of multi-track recording. A 4 piece band was now able to record with 24 tracks. On stage, there would be one rhythm guitar and the lead guitar playing a solo. In the studio, 5 rhythm guitar tracks and 10 background vocals were mixed flawlessly under the pristine 4th take of the solo. Records sounded better than ever.

In the late 70's and 80's, synthesizers were used to duplicate horn and string sections. It was extremely practical to have one keyboardist take the place of many horn and string players. Most musicians realized that the synth didn't always have the sonic quality of the "real thing", but it was close enough for the general public. The live sound was quickly approaching the quality of the recorded sound.

Later, sequencers and backing tracks became all the rage. This was quite a shift. Up until this point, someone had to actually play the horn and string parts on a synth. Now, sequencers and tracks were running pre-recorded music. Suddenly, the local bar band was able to sequence an entire night of material. A 3 piece band sounded like an orchestra. A mediocre pianist was now able to pre-record more demanding musical passages, playing only the simpler parts on stage. Additional percussion and vocals were at your fingertips in this brave new world.

The 90's ushered in the age of Pro Tools and other methods of digitally fixing every mistake in the studio. In this era, every drummer is perfectly in time, every singer in tune. An individual performance in the studio can be imperfect. (I'm being kind. Don't get used to it.) These less than stellar performances on any instrument can be quantized and corrected by the hand of a talented producer pushing a button. This admittedly is an oversimplified explanation, but it's the same idea as creating a 25 page word document and then using spell and grammar check to fix all the errors. It's essentially your writing, but you've had a lot of help.

That is not the end of the story. All of this progress in the recording studio has now made its way to the stage. Synths led to samplers and sequencers, which led to backing tracks which resulted in a boat load of major artists lip syncing to pre-recorded music. Many of these tools are affordable to the novice with a home studio as well as the neighborhood wedding band. Some look at this as progress. Others look at it as cheating. In fact, it's neither. It's just technology.

You can't blame some computer geek in the Silicon Valley for inventing programs and chips to make this stuff available to us. You can't blame the local band for taking every opportunity to sound bigger and better. Discussing the pros and cons of the latest software and technology is a slippery slope. As a self proclaimed dinosaur, I always see George Harrison's guitar solos as legendary because his sound and style are such integral parts of the Beatles songs. I spent many hours learning those solos note for note. That was a big part of my musical training. I felt that playing those parts faithfully when performing in local clubs was my job as a working musician. The thought of sampling Harrison's solo seems criminal. Yet, bands do it at the local club and the audience isn't aware of what is really happening. They see a guitarist on the stage.

They hear a guitar solo. They come to the obvious conclusion that the guitarist is playing the guitar solo. The audience is wrong.

I always have mixed feelings when I'm using pre-recorded music in a live environment. However, I constantly use Pro Tools in the studio to cut and paste choruses. In essence, I sing one chorus and simply paste it in the song 3 or 4 times. Then, we sometimes use pitch correction to fix the flat or sharp notes. (Honestly, I don't always use the pitch correction. Sometimes, a performance loses some character when it's too perfect.) I am knowingly contradicting myself here. I wrestle with the idea of "fooling" the live audience with backing tracks, but sleep like a baby after copying, cutting and pitch correcting in the studio.

I said this discussion can be a slippery slope. Is it cheating that bands use all this technology? Is it acceptable to call yourself a musician and a singer if you're not playing music or singing? Is it OK simply because everyone else is doing it? If I use this technology, even some of the time, am I a hypocrite for raising these questions?

BOTTOM LINE:

These are tough questions. In baseball, illegal use of steroids has tarnished many reputations and compromised the entire sport because these drugs artificially enhance a player's performance. However, the musical questions we raise here are ethical, not legal. It's not illegal to lip sync. The question now becomes, is it unethical to ask anyone to buy a ticket and wait in line to see an artist NOT SING? In 1990, the pop duo Milli Vanilli were stripped of their Grammy when it was discovered that they had not sung on their own record and were lip syncing in live performances. My, how things have changed.

I have used pre-recorded tracks as a matter of practicality. I would use a mandolin track on one song rather than bring a mandolin player on a road gig to perform only one song in a 60 minute set. However, I would not pre-record a Van Halen-esque guitar solos and make believe I was playing them live. Is it enhancement or deception? You make the call.

THE IT FACTOR

You just left the Aromadome where you and 20,000 other fans saw your favorite band, Remnants of Phlegm, perform the greatest show in the history of music. Everything about the performance was fantastic. They sang well. They played well. More than that, they had that indescribable thing that separates them from the others. They had "it".

We know "it" when we see it. We know "it" when we hear it. A few of us have it. Most of us don't. All of us want it. Can we get it? Can we rent "it"?

So many questions and so little patience on my part! The IT FACTOR is a source of great mystery. Why does an average singer knock the audience dead with his performance when a better technical singer goes over like a lead balloon? What makes a performer endearing to the audience? It's usually because he or she has that special something known as "IT." What is IT and where does it come from? Is IT animal, vegetable or mineral? Let's examine this mystery.

Any artist that is comfortable onstage immediately has a leg up on the competition. When the artist is confident, the audience feels it. The person onstage is confident in his ability and at ease in front of an audience.

Confidence is big part of IT.

Confidence should be put on a sliding scale here. For instance, an entertainer can be confident about his guitar playing but not his dancing ability. When he takes a solo, he's playing from his heart, but when he is asked to perform a few simple dance steps, he feels silly. Some players lose all their bravado when they have to sing a little background vocal part. Some great musicians have a lot of trouble just talking to the audience for a moment in between songs. These individuals all have a "partial it". I know it sounds funny, but they need to get all of it. They have great potential, but their talent needs to be maximized.

Why does the great guitarist feel so silly when dancing? It's because dancing is his "personal kryptonite". It's the thing that makes you lose your power. You are edgy and nervous in the first set because you are dreading having to try that little dance step in the second set. It scares you and distracts you. It saps your energy and doesn't allow focusing and being in the moment. Job # 1 in obtaining the IT FACTOR is identifying your "personal kryptonite." What is the element of performing that knocks you off your game? Surprisingly, it may not be the element that you do worst. It's just the one that makes you uncomfortable.

As a lead singer, I am always thrilled when the backing vocals kick in on the chorus of a song. I live to hear the background oohs and ahhs on the bridge of the Motown classics. I worked with a drummer for years who was reluctant to sing harmony. He shied away from the mic when asked to sing, apologizing every night, saying his voice is too weak and he's flat on that high harmony. I had to tell him over and over that he sounded great. I wasn't saying that just to make him feel better. Everyone thought he sang very well. His lack of confidence clouded his perception.

This drummer has to find a way to get over the fear of singing. He will have to put himself out there and make a few mistakes. He may have to practice at home. He must get to a place in his head where he can sing his parts with the same conviction with which he plays the drums. He is fully capable of hitting the notes. It seems that everyone knows that but him. Voice may never be his strongest instrument. He may not sing at the same level as he plays drums but he should perform both with the same conviction and confidence. That is an essential part of getting the IT Factor.

Upon getting a handle on your personal kryptonite, you now are ready to go to the next step. This one hurts a little. Now you have to identify what it is you think you do well. Your band members and fans might not agree with you. Let's explore this a little deeper.

DANCING IN THE KITCHEN

I wonder what you are expecting to extract from this chapter. What knowledge could you possibly cull from pages with this title? Dancing in the kitchen is a phrase I made up, referring to two of my weakest points.

I can't cook. I truly do not know how to roast a chicken or make a pot of coffee.

I can't dance. Not a step. Never could and probably never will.

If I were to combine these non-skills, I would be at my absolute worst. I can't imagine any good coming out of my dancing in the kitchen. I can easily imagine a torrent of burned sushi and pulled hamstrings.

I have come across many entertainers who insist on dancing in the kitchen. In the chapter called THE IT FACTOR, we looked at a Musician's Personal Kryptonite. We talked about realizing your fears and overcoming them, in essence, accentuating the positive and eliminating the negative. As an artist, you should constantly strive to expand your horizons and push the envelope. However, you must realize that there is a time and place for this growth.

Those that are fortunate enough to have "IT" are ahead of the game. They probably don't need to work as hard on the details of stage presence and performance. Those who are enlightened enough to understand which aspects of their game need work will probably prevail. They will take care of business and refine their act.

There will still be others that are dancing in the kitchen. These folks insist upon making the same mistakes over and over. They just keep doing what they do worst. They have no ear for harmony, yet they insist upon singing. It's week # 6 of your jazz trio gig, but the sax player still insists on playing those extra 3 notes at the end of the song. The other guitarist in your acoustic duo thinks it's cool to play the "substitution" chords he learned yesterday. Someone has to tell him that all he's doing is substituting the wrong chords for the correct chords.

These musicians never seem to "get it" no matter how many times they are told. If you are one of these players, you need to be realistic. You also need to respect the craft and the art form. The sax player needs to end the song when everyone else ends the song. The guitarist needs to be tasteful about his choices, as opposed to just throwing in the latest lessons from his music book. In both these cases, the music is diminished. The band and the patrons deserve better. It is an atrocity to be so selfish and self-serving as to insult the audience.

The previous chapter ended with this paragraph:

"Upon getting a handle on your personal kryptonite, you now are ready to go to the next step. This one hurts a little. Now you have to identify what it is you think you do well. Your band members and fans might not agree with you. Let's explore this a little deeper."

I thought it was important to repeat those lines because what you think you do well and what you actually do well might be two different things. Many times, a singer rehearses his part and really thinks he's got a handle on it.

He doesn't, but you found out too late.

Our fearless lead singer, Brock Harley, has a good voice. He's not a bad guitarist. He's a good guy on many levels. Brock considers himself somewhat of a ladies man. He thinks of himself as sexy and darned near irresistible. We know this because each night, he walks up to the microphone and says, "Hi, I'm Brock Harley. I'm sexy and darned near irresistible." Some think he's kidding. We know he's not.

Brock takes the stage with great confidence. The band sounds great. He begins to charm the audience. He's doing well, as evidenced by the packed dance floor and the smiling women. Brock begins to groove and sway. The smiling women fuel his fire. He wiggles a little. They smile more, so he wiggles more, misconstruing their laughter at his inability to dance. Everyone is in on the joke except Brock. It is then that Brock breaks the 11th Commandment. THOU SHALT NOT USE THE PELVIC THRUST.

Brock is unaware that he is dancing in the kitchen. Brock is equally unaware of his ability to repel women. He swears that his spasms are an integral component of the show and therefore takes every opportunity to get down and get funky. The band wishes he would get down and just stay down.

In the first example in the previous chapter, the drummer actually sings better than he thinks he does. He needs to be encouraged. It might be a good idea to record a show in order to prove to him just how good he sounds. Before you pack up the camera, grab some footage of old Brock for his edification. If a picture paints a thousand words, imagine how much uncomfortable conversation you could avoid.

This process is good for all of us. We blue collar musicians have a little saying. "Everybody sucks at something." Don't sweat it. There will always be aspects of your musicianship that you want to expand. You may want to take piano lessons even though you've been a percussionist for the last 10 years. That's great. Realize (please, please realize) that you may not be up to the task of playing piano in public for a while. Consider (please, please consider) the rest of the band. Understand your place in the scheme of things. You have to crawl before you walk. If you weren't born with the IT Factor, work on it. You may obtain it someday. Meanwhile, take baby steps and stop dancing in the kitchen.

BOTTOM LINE:

Pick your spots carefully. Don't attempt to stretch and grow at the expense of your audience. Do your homework at home, not onstage.

Dear Diary #3,

Last night, All 3 of us arrived at the club at 8:45. The club owner immediately informed us that the start time was 9 PM, not 9:30. We had 15 minutes to load in, park our cars, set up and sound check. We were also meeting Donnie, the drummer, for the first time.

The place was crowded, making load in somewhat difficult. All 3 band members were hustling furiously to get things together. We didn't have enough time to talk about a set list. We had to set up and go.

The first set was rough. Intros and endings were weak. Donnie was guessing at some of the tempos. We were all struggling. We were all frustrated. We got through set # 1 and walked off the stage looking like a football team that was losing 28-0 at halftime.

I wasn't feeling good about it. I got mad for a minute and then I calmed down and tried to think it through. All of us want to make this gig work. Two of us are trying so hard to cue the drummer that we're not able to focus on our own performance. The drummer is uncomfortable because he's used to playing some of these tunes in different keys and tempos with his regular band.

I spoke up. "OK, we're all competent musicians. Let's put a little faith in each other. Let's each do our own job and let the other do his job. We'll all watch for hand signals and cues for solos and endings. We'll listen to each other and lock in the groove and keep the volume at a manageable level. Let's relax and have some fun. We're making each other too uptight."

The other two players thought about it for a second. Then, we all laughed. We all agreed that we were our own worst enemy. It became a vicious cycle. The more uptight we got, the more mistakes we made. The more mistakes we made, the more uptight we got. The solution was to obviously get back to just playing music and having a good time.

The rest of the night was great. There were still a handful of mistakes. So what! It's a live performance. A gig is more than musical notes. We had fun. The crowd had fun. We sounded good and tight because we allowed each other to do what we do best.

This was a great lesson to learn, or learn again. You shouldn't put too much pressure on the band. It rarely makes for a better gig. I am admittedly stating the obvious many times in this book, but there are some gig fundamentals that need to be reinforced. You can't expect the audience to have a good time if the band isn't having a good time. Your job is to make it fun for everyone. That's not a bad job!

BURN, BABY, BURN OUT

It's hard to imagine burning out playing music. How can you get tired of doing a job that everyone wants? Playing music is the greatest job in the world, but like every job, it can burn you out if you're not careful. If you get tired of a certain band you can join another band, but what happens when you burn out on being a musician?

A job can get depressing when one goes to the same office, sits at the same desk and does the same thing everyday. Musical burnout is somewhat different. Very few musicians work the same club week after week. In fact, a house gig is often viewed as the ultimate in club work, as it is the closest thing to job security music has to offer. For most players, there is a constant change of scene. It's not the same daily commute or the work routine that burns out a musician.

It's the sense of failure. You don't burn out from a sense of too much satisfaction, now do you? It's that feeling of being stuck. I've seen it happen many times. The gigs, the rehearsals and the auditions pile up and run together in your head. You realize that had you spent the last 4 years doing something else, you'd be further along. In that time, your little brother graduated from college, your girlfriend got 2 promotions and your lazy friend from high school opened his own restaurant. You look around one day and feel as if you're stuck in the mud and the world is passing you by.

For these last 4 years, your nephew, your neighbor and everyone else has been telling you how lucky you are to be doing what you love. They envy you for following your dream. You don't feel so lucky. In fact, sometimes you envy them for having a family, a house and a new car. They have security and some money in the bank. They have health insurance, paid vacations and OH MY GOD WHAT THE HELL HAVE I BEEN DOING WITH MY LIFE FOR THE LAST 31 YEARS!!

Everyone please return to your seats. Uncle Billy had a little emotional tremor that seems to have passed. As I was saying, musical burn out happens all the time. Sure, you can find yourself in a rut in most any job, but most day jobs offer steady pay and benefits. Most musicians burn out on club gigs, quit playing music, get a real job and enjoy their memories. Others try to dull the pain of burn out with alcohol and drugs. Some just trudge on with their misery and continue to burn. That last bunch is no fun at all.

I choose to keep playing. I have always played in several bands simultaneously. I have done 3 gigs a day and also taken long vacations. I have packed up and moved my life to several parts of the United States. I have written and co-written, recorded and re-recorded my own music as well as others and will continue to do so.

I have never once given up on my true identity as a musician. I worked some terrible day jobs just to pay the rent. I drove a truck but never referred to myself as a truck driver. I never felt like anything other than a musician. Philosophically speaking, these jobs all contributed to my life experience and thus, my career. When things get tough in music, I think back to some of my awful part-time jobs. I loaded food in a freezer, wearing a hooded parka in 15 degrees Fahrenheit. I mixed cement in the summer. I was a courier in Los Angeles traffic. That was the worst job I ever had until I was "promoted" to dispatcher. Dispatcher was not a promotion. It was more like a death sentence. That didn't last long.

Through it all, I remained a musician at heart. That is what kept me going. That is what kept me from burning out. I played in many bands in many places. I did my best and moved on. I learned when to hold 'em and when to fold 'em, as Kenny Rogers sang. When money was tight, I spent less and sometimes got a part time job. When I outgrew a band, I gave notice. I learned to breathe deep. I learned to let go. I never reached stardom but never once felt like a failure. In all these years, I can honestly say musical burn out has not been an issue for me. Life for me is simple. I play basketball during the day and music at night. I have a woman who loves me.

Throw in a pizza and I call it Heaven. That's really all there is to it.

NOBODY WALKS IN LA

Guitarist wanted. Must have reliable transpo.

The above ad appears in every Los Angeles music paper. That's because a car is an essential part of living in LA. New York, Boston and London have public transportation. LA has it, but nobody uses it. I guess it's transportation but it's not very public. If you don't have a car, you better have a girlfriend because you're going to need a ride.

As a musician, you can't be too picky about transpo. You drive whatever car you can afford. This means it is a vehicle that no one else in the world would drive. Don't be ashamed. You're a musician and no one will judge you by the car you drive. In fact, if your band rocks, people will think your car is cool and they'll love you. I know guys that drive old checker cabs from the 60's and another that drives a hearse. One guy still has the longhorns of a Brahma bull on the grill of his 25 year old mint condition Cadillac. Oops. These are bad examples. These are just cool cars. The guys who drive them are idiots and nobody likes them.

Let's start over. No one will judge you by the car you drive. Everyone understands that you're a struggling musician. You suffer for your art and can't be shackled by possessions. Good thing!

The band cars are always easy to spot in the parking lot. They are right next to the club owner's new Porsche. The musician's car is usually a "Cyclops", meaning only one headlight is working. The driver's door is a different color. The Nine Inch Nails bumper sticker is holding the trunk closed. The 2 weeks worth of Styrofoam coffee cups in the backseat serve as soundproofing for the muffler that does very little muffling.

The local car wash calls the HAZMAT team to clean the interior. Something is crawling in the cup holder. The brakes are so far gone, their picture appears on the side of a milk carton. The passenger window sticks and the horn won't work below 70 degrees. A roll of duct tape doubles as the spare tire, under which is a tuxedo jacket. Last but not least, the dashboard hosts a 14,000 watt, 26 speaker surround sound Ipod ready, 75 CD changer, satellite radio, wi-fi internet, flat screen mother of all entertainment centers complete with lighting trusses for enhanced interactive performances.

I've seen these cars for years. I must admit, I really admire the guys who drive them. My first thought is that they should spend less money on the sound system and more on the brakes and tires. After further review, I realize that these are the musicians who truly walk the walk. Music is their top priority. They don't care about the look of the car. (Apparently, they don't care about the safety, either.) These musicians surround themselves with music. They often work 2 or even 3 jobs in order to pay for this luxury.

If they applied that type of commitment to my band, I'd consider myself lucky. I'd be honored to have them on the team.

I'd drive myself to rehearsal, though.

BOTTOM LINE:

If it gets you to the gig, it's a great car.

I THINK, THEREFORE, I JAM

I have been a member of the house band for several jam nights around Los Angeles. I have the scars to prove it. Nothing will burn you out faster than playing Stormy Monday 3 times in one set. That would never happen at a gig. That only happens at a jam night.

Let me explain the basics of a jam night. It usually takes place in a club on an "off-night", such as a Monday or Tuesday. Musicians get together in a loose and casual atmosphere and play music. They "jam." There is no song list. There are no charts. There are a lot of guitar solos. Stacks of guitar solos. Much of the time, there are several players who meet for the first time onstage. It can be fun, exciting and a little nerve wracking for the uninitiated.

There is usually a house band that gets things pointed in the right direction. While the band plays, musicians sign up for their turn to play. On any given night, the list will be 10 deep at every instrument. The band leader calls up players one or two at a time to sit in with the band. Each player gets to perform 2 or 3 songs before handing over his spot to the next player. Soon, the house band is at the bar and the stage is full of musicians hoping the drummer knows how to end the tune. Often, it's great. Sometimes it's just plain terrible. It's always an experience.

Experience is the word on which we need to concentrate. If you are a young player just getting started, you can use all the experience you can get. Jam nights can be a musical boot camp. You learn to fly by the seat of your pants. You can be playing with 3 different drummers in 20 minutes. You'll undoubtedly have to sing a song that's not in your key. You'll be forced to play on someone else's rig. You'll have to follow along on songs you've never heard before. There will be tough situations, but it's all fantastic training.

I have always been an R&B and classic rock guy. I have never been much of a jazz bassist. In order to broaden my musical vocabulary, I sometimes go to a jazz jam. It is always refreshing to play with a drummer using brushes and a pianist playing an acoustic piano. It's easy to be intimidated when you step out of your comfort zone. You don't have to feel intimidated. Feel humbled. Feel enriched. You walked out of that club with a little more knowledge. Just pray that nobody plays the bebop version of Stormy Monday.

As you take your craft more seriously, you may want to stretch out even more. Paying gigs can be hard to find. Jam nights are in abundance. Make it a point to go to different clubs to play with and hear different players. As the house bandleader, I had often noticed a lot of the same players showing up and playing the same tunes week after week. They would seek out the same guys each night. Certainly, that's no crime. After all, it's supposed to be loose. However, I would suggest that you keep the big picture in mind. It's a jam, not a gig. Give it some thought. You're supposed to try new things and step out a little. Get crazy and play a bluesy version of HELLAGOOD or a punk version of a classic Sinatra tune. Why not? That stuff never happens on a gig. It only happens at a jam night.

BOTTOM LINE:

Every musician should go to at least one jam before they die.

Beware. One too many jam nights might be the death of you.

STUDIO WORK: THE ART
OF SONIC SPELUNKING

The recording studio is the place where you immortalize your suckage. You start with an awful song. Your terrible band performs these songs in a recording studio where every horrible note will be captured for all of time. This will happen to you time and time again unless you learn from your mistakes.

Looks like I got here just in time! I completely understand this conundrum. I have written some of those awful songs and performed with several of those awful bands. While in these bands, we pooled our money and rented a "good" recording studio in hope that some engineer would turn several blue and red knobs, causing magic songs and hundred dollar bills to fly out of the machine. I was never fortunate enough to get those results, but it isn't as far fetched as it sounds.

Given enough time and money, almost anyone can make a great recording. Technology compensates for a lack of talent in many cases. If you have the time, the tools and the money, you can tune every note and quantize the beat of every drum. (It's a great gig for an engineer who gets paid by the hour).

The idea of spending so much time and money on recording is impractical for most of us, but you should understand that it happens all too often. It can make a star out of no talent, good for nothing, brainless bimbo who never played an instrument or wrote a note of music and has to lip sync onstage because of the aforementioned lack of talent. (Geez, I hope she needs a bass player.) In essence, the big budget recording made a lot of money for someone with little to offer. The hundred dollar bills did in fact fly out of that machine.

The $100,000 recording should not be the measuring stick here. You no doubt have considerably less money and time. You need to maximize both. Our goal here is to refine your talent as a musician and a songwriter and use the technology as a tool, not a life preserver. That's a politically correct way of telling you to actually learn how to play and sing before you record.

As a songwriter, your job is to write the song that matters to you. Draw on your musical influences and personal experiences. The song can be a love song or a comedic parody, but it should be a personal message or expression. This sentiment needs to be captured in the studio and conveyed in the recording.

Some rehearsal and preproduction will help you and the band get the basic feel and vibe for the song. This preproduction will pave the way for plenty of spontaneity in the recording session. Each player will have a blueprint for the song and therefore a sense of space in the music. This will allow each member to round out the tune with drum fills and guitar licks which will result in a real song.

Great recording can be done in the garage or the spare room. Producing your own music for TV, film and your band's promo kit can be accomplished in a home studio. Great equipment rarely fixes a bad song. Write the song that matters to you. Don't write the song you think will sell. That almost never works. Be creative and put your heart and soul into it. Do it with the understanding that it might never make a dime. Some people don't understand that concept. I play basketball every day. I play as hard as I can all the time. I know I'll never play in the NBA, but I play because I love the game. That's all the motivation I need. If you take that same approach towards your musical composition, you'll probably write some good songs.

I'm not about to say too much more about songwriting because it is a far too subjective process. Everyone writes from a different perspective with a different technique. I'm not giving any advice about how to write a song other than to say that it should be one that matters to you.

The music and lyrics probably won't change too drastically during the recording. The recording, however, will take on a life of its own. As you get into the preproduction, you decide to change the tempo a little. In the studio, the piano player accidentally goes to a C instead of an A minor and you love it! The lyric sheet slips off the music stand and your impromptu 4 bar scat is absolute magic. It's a mixed bag of carefully written charts and happy accidents. The more you record, the more comfortable you will be with the process.

It's easy to be overwhelmed in the studio. That's natural. Breathe deep and focus. Use your head. You might have to be your own producer for a while. That's good news. You'll get a first hand look at how many decisions have to be made. You'll find out in a hurry what matters most and what must be sacrificed. You'll realize that hiring a 5 piece string section was a noble concept, but might not be in the budget for now. Practicality is suddenly your new best friend.

You thought you had things pretty well mapped out, but the best laid plans of mice and men oft times go astray in the studio. That dobro just doesn't sound as good as you had hoped. The bassist's falsetto always sounded great in the clubs, but it's not working for you now. That's ok. This will force you to be creative and find another way to make the tune work. The band is momentarily lost in this cave, so you will then do a little sonic spelunking.

You'll experiment, you'll explore, you'll screw up a few times and you'll come out with a great record that's a little different than you expected.

BOTTOM LINE:

As a blue collar songwriter, walk into the studio with a good song. We know that "good" is difficult to define. So is spelunking! You must believe in the song and feel it's your best work. If the song speaks to you, you'll perform it well and record it well, allowing your song to speak to someone else. The job of everyone in the studio is to make the best record possible. Get 'er done!

PRODUCERS ARE CONTROL FREAKS

If you are a producer, you best be smiling as you read the title of this chapter. If you are smiling, then you have accepted the fact that I am right. If you are not, I guess you'll never hire me again.

The producer is the person responsible for walking into a room with an idea and walking out with a record. The songwriter wrote the song and the band played it, but the producer made the whole thing happen with a healthy dose of suggestions, critiques and the occasional high 5. You need to be a control freak when producing.

I get along fine with control freaks. I actually prefer to work for control freaks. Being a bit of a CF myself, I realize that things usually get done when someone like me is in charge. I know how that sounds, but I truly believe it.

A control freak is a person who attempts to dictate how everything around them is done. He sees his way as beneficial or even necessary, believing that others are incapable of handling matters properly. A control freak feels this is due to his superior intellect and aptitude. I agree with the above definitions. Producers use words such as "harmonics" and "quantize". Musicians use words like "yeah" and "sandwich". There you have it.

I don't necessarily think of "control freak" as a derogatory term. In my experience, a producer takes the bull by the horns. He sees the big picture and has the clearest vision of how to reach the finish line. I have had the pleasure of working with some well known and well respected producers in some of the great studios. I have also done some of my own producing in several home studios. In any case, the producer is the one with his ear on the speaker and his eye on the clock. Players must respect the fact that he is constantly multi-tasking. The goal is to get the project finished on time and on budget, while attaining the lofty goal of giving the band the record they want.

It takes time and energy to make a great recording. That's a given. This does not mean that the band should take 2 hours of studio time deciding which hi hat would sound best. This is where the producer might step in and say, "Enough!", and choose one. The drummer will feel wounded for the moment. Later, the entire band will realize that the control freak made the right decision. The record sounds great and the hi hat is not an issue.

A producer should dictate how everything in the studio is done. He can certainly listen to suggestions from the band. He takes all the creative input and filters it down, making the final decisions as to how to proceed on technical and musical issues. If he has to explain himself on each decision, the recording process will take forever. Microphone choices, drum fills and melodic changes are all arrows in his quiver and he will choose the appropriate one when ready to steady his bow and hit the bull's eye. OK, please tell me you're laughing at that!! Quivers and arrows, my ass! Trust the producer to make these choices. Period.

BOTTOM LINE:

I hope I have made the case that being a control freak/producer is a good thing. If not, I believe I was just crossed off the Christmas lists of Peter Asher and Michael Lloyd.

NAMM, BAM, THANK YOU, MA'AM

The NAMM show is a huge music convention that takes place twice a year. Thousands attend these conventions, but how many know what NAMM stands for? It stands for the National Association of Megalo-Maniacs. It's largely a "check me out" convention. I go all the time.

The NAMM show has been coming to LA for many years. I have been a regular since 1994. NAMM actually stands for the National Association of Music Merchants, a place where companies from all over the world showcase the latest and greatest inventions in musical gear and technology. They do their best to get retailers to buy these products in order to sell them to the public. The merchants pull out all the stops to make a good impression. They rent huge booths to display guitars, amps and drums. They use gargantuan projection screens for software demonstrations. They hook up multi-colored floodlights to illuminate their products on pedestals. When all that inevitably fails, they hire pretty girls.

These pretty girls are models, not employees of the merchant. They know nothing of the product and are unable to give you any useful information about the company or its services. They are merely there to catch the eye of the male consumers and invite them into their web. It is a highly successful strategy, as a lot of this useless crap gets sold every year.

Another successful strategy is to get a superstar to endorse the merchant's newest piece of musical doo-doo. When a no name such as Bill Cinque plugs in the Phantasmo-Guitar and plays BACK IN BLACK, no one at NAMM so much as turns their head. However, when young Mr. Rippey Jeans, with so much hair product that his head received a formal invitation from OPEC, plays a blues riff on the same guitar, he gets a crowd, an endorsement deal and a hook up with 2 of those stupid models.

I'm not complaining. I have an endorsement deal and, well, one out of three ain't bad. It is interesting to watch how a company tries to push the product by luring big name celebrities but the big names don't necessarily need the new gear. Some companies fall all over themselves taking photos of Mr. Rippey Jeans using their newest guitar and amp. Will Mr. Rippey Jeans ever play the Phantasmo-Guitar on stage or in the studio? We'll see about that.

If the working class musician is lucky enough to get an endorsement deal, chances are he or she will be using that gear onstage. The blue collar guy is proud to display his endorsement and more than happy to advertise. In fact, you usually can't shut him up. He'll be all too pleased with himself for getting a drum kit for 40% off retail and will tell anyone who will listen (and many that won't) about every detail of the endorsement deal. I know I do.

Endorsements can be great for both parties. For example, the player gets a great guitar at a huge discount, sometimes free. The company gets a high profile player to use the guitar on stage and in video. The players are endorsers, as they are endorsing the product. These players almost always credit the company they endorse on any recordings. The company lists the artist on their website and often in their advertisements. That's how it works.

The NAMM Show is a great place to network with companies and individuals. You get to meet some of your idols. You get to speak with representatives whose companies are on the cutting edge of technology. You get to play with toys that won't even be in the stores for 2 months.

It gets pretty noisy, but it can be a lot of fun.

BOTTOM LINE:

Experience the NAMM show if you get the chance. It's not open to the public. You have to be a vendor, artist, exhibitor or a guest of one of the merchants in order to attend. I have had the privilege of having endorsement deals with several companies, allowing me access to the NAMM show. I recently became friends with Chris D, who works for FISHMAN ELECTRONICS, a fantastic company which makes fantastic products. Chris is a fantastic guy. Am I calling the company fantastic simply because they issued me NAMM passes for the last 3 years? No. It's because they issued my entire band NAMM passes for the last 3 years!! Are they fantastic or what?? I hope Chris doesn't get in any trouble for this because I'm hoping for a gig with the Los Angeles Symphony. I'm counting on 127 NAMM passes for next year.

IMAGINARY LETTERS FROM THE IMAGINARY FANS OF MY IMAGINARY ADVICE COLUMN

Dear Bill,
I was fired from the Madison Square Garden maintenance staff when the foreman deemed my technical skills questionable. I was found responsible for the infamous thermostat mishap of 1982 which resulted in an event that has since become known as the STEAMCAPADES, naming me Public Enemy #1 in ZAMBONI MONTHLY.

For the last 26 years I have been sleeping on my sister's couch, teaching myself to play the spoons. Do you think I have a career in music?
Sincerely,
In Time but Out of Work

Dear In Time,
It sounds to me as though you have made some brave choices in your life. Clearly, you are selfless, as you have chosen not to be a burden on your sister and elected to stay on the couch as opposed to curled up at the foot of her bed. I hope she appreciates your sacrifice.

Your innate sense of the unconventional is at its zenith, as you opted for the instrument known fondly as the "rhythm of the night." The spoon, the most percussive of the silverware family, is as practical as it is musical. After a strenuous recording session with the Flatware Philharmonic of Greater Fresno, you alone will be able to use your "axe" to eat tapioca pudding. Try that, Gene Krupa!!

My advice to you is reach for the stars and be the man of music with a dull edge but a bright future!

Dear Bill,
I have sold millions of records. My autobiography is # 1 on the New York Times Best Seller List. My rock opera is the biggest hit on Broadway. I have a mansion in the Hollywood Hills and a penthouse in Manhattan. I drive a different Mercedes every day of the week and date several supermodels. Yet, I'm not happy. What should I do?
Richie Filth

Dear Richie,
Go fuck yourself.
Sincerely,
Everyone on the planet!!

Dear Bill,

Who the Hell do you think you are telling other people about music? I've seen your act several times. You suck! You're a lousy singer, a terrible bassist and a total ass! You are an embarrassment to musicians everywhere. Your own band talks about you behind your back. They can't stand you. I can't stand you!
Sincerely,
Unsigned.

Dear Mom,

This is the third letter this week. It's not funny anymore. It's hurtful and it's nonproductive. Dr. Kleinman says this type of transference is common among unfulfilled women of your age. We can talk about this more on Tuesday when I drop off my laundry.

Dear Bill,
I have been taking bass lessons for 8 years, but am hampered by the fact that I have 2 pinkies and no thumb on my right hand. Any recommendations?
Slapless In Seattle

Dear Slapless,
Play congas.

Dear Bill,
I just celebrated my 146th birthday. I'm the oldest musician on the planet, which of course means I'm also the oldest waiter. I recently saw this ad online on THE MUSICIANS CONTACT SERVICE.
Wanted: accordionist who doubles on trombone. Must have pro gear, light travel. Must be under 117 years of age. No osteoporosis, please! Valid passport.

This seems like my dream gig, but I'm not sure how to respond. Please help me. I mean, really help me. Forget the ad. I've fallen and I can't get up.
Hurry!
Kane Walker

Dear Kane,
Lie still until the ambulance arrives. Meanwhile, I'll address your musical situation. First of all, you seem to be intelligent and charismatic. A man of your wisdom would be a tremendous asset to any band over the age of 80.

These guys should understand that ageism is wrong. It's a cancerous prejudice that undermines the global brotherhood of the musical community.

For them to openly announce that you won't be accepted based solely on the fact that you are older than the absolutely arbitrary age of 117 is preposterous. Would it be acceptable to say that no men are allowed in the Go-Go's? That no Caucasians be allowed in Earth, Wind and Fire? No Breeders in the Gay Men's Choir?

You should take charge of this matter. March right up to their door (use the ramp) and demand an audition that is fairly and squarely based on talent and not on age. Once you start kickin' that squeezebox old school, the young whippersnappers will understand what you bring to the table. When you show them what it was like to play that slide "T-Bone" back in the day, they'll sit up and take notice.

Knock'em out, Kane Baby!

NOTE:

I realize that this started out as silly, but is now taking on real meaning for a 51 year old musician. Boy is my face red.

THE JAZZ GIG

By far the most demanding gig of all, the jazz gig has the potential to be musically challenging and spiritually rewarding for the musician. The audience is often challenged to stay awake and upright. You get the chance to "stretch" and use your "chops." The audience gets a chance to text message the babysitter while watching THE ENGLISH PATIENT with the sound off. You use terms such as "straight ahead" and "fusion" even though you have no clue what they mean. Your wife has no idea why she agreed to sit there for the third Tuesday in a row.

There are several keys to doing a proper jazz gig.

1. You must always wear a jacket and tie. For most musicians, this means you have to borrow your little brother's communion suit. I usually sidestep this problem by going to the really expensive restaurant down the street. They have a dress code. I walk in wearing a collared shirt. The maitre'd hands me a jacket and tie, insisting that I wear it in order to be seated. I accept, casually walk out the back door and return to the jazz club and do the gig, wearing this lime green jacket and plaid tie. My outfit is the loudest thing onstage.

2. Start the first set by just playing random notes out of tune and out of time for 12 minutes. Then say, "Thank you. That was Somewhere Over the Rainbow." Nobody in that audience will admit that they didn't recognize it. You'll get a standing ovation.

3. Never chug a beer at a jazz gig. It looks undignified. Sip some chardonnay instead. If you really want to impress, shoot heroin.
4. Deny any knowledge of current pop music. Any talk of Top 40 radio tunes will make you sound like a sell out and the jazz Mafia will take out a hit on you. They wouldn't be stupid enough to hire any "local talent" to do the job. They'll fly in a vibraphonist from Chicago. Keep your mouth shut and watch your back.
5. After you've repeated the 3 real jazz tunes you know, play all your old Boy Scout campfire songs using major 7ths and minor 9ths. When that fails, play the entire PUDDLE OF MUDD catalog as a samba.

THE COUNTRY GIG

My good friend Cary is one of the truly great country guitar players. My first piece of advice to any county musician would be to get a gig with Cary as soon as possible. Of course, that might not be so easy for many of you, so I have a PLAN B, detailed below. As in most cases, I have thought of everything.

Don't try to impress country players in Nashville or Memphis with attitude or name dropping. It doesn't work. These folks are immune to the typical buzz words and talk of the next big thing. This holds true for the country musicians in Los Angeles as well. The only Hollywood bull that interests these guys is the mechanical one at the Saddle Ranch Chop House on Sunset. I can't figure it out. Is there some sort of anti-hype emulsifier in their chewing tobacco? Logic would tell me that these players are only interested in the music. Only interested in the music? This is a foreign concept to the rest of us, for sure.

Apparently, if these county folks are holding an audition, they are looking strictly for talent. This will be a stumbling block because you have very little talent. You must be creative in order to get this gig. You must use your head.

Wow! This is getting tougher by the minute.

First, you must talk like them. Learn to be a mimic, a vocal chameleon. (You've been a snake to your band mates, a toad to your girlfriend and you'll probably spend your golden years as a lounge lizard, so you might as well stay in the reptilian groove. The chameleon thing should be easy). Say "y'all" and "howdy" every chance you get. This will endear you to them. Start every sentence with, "Weeeeell, I'll tell ya, boys" and finish each sentence with "yes siree, Bob." These phrases will make you sound authentic, hiding any trace of your Teaneck, New Jersey lineage.

When the musical director asks where you live, say "just passin' through." This will make you sound grizzled and road worthy. Make use of accessories such as bandanas and toothpicks, but go easy on things such as boots and hats. Remember, we don't want to be conspicuous.

Refer to the icons as "Johnny, Willie and Patsy." If you have to use their last names, you will be found out as a fraud and the fiddle player will take you out behind the barn for a whoopin' with a hickory switch.

These clever skills should get you the country gig without ever playing a note at the audition. Rather than baffling them with double speak and quotes from Variety, you've blinded them with down home charm and affability. Now, you're a full-time member of the Star Spangled Blue Moon of Kentucky Saddle Sore All Stars, and they don't even know what instrument you play.

When you finally have to do your first country gig, repeat the only 3 real country tunes you know. Then, play the entire PUDDLE OF MUDD catalog on pedal steel. Be sure to take the harmonica player quail hunting after the last set.

BOTTOM LINE

I feel comfortable making these generalizations as I am both a born city slicker and an honorary redneck, granting me immunity as I poke fun at both. I am truly that rare combination of Studio 54 and Hee Haw which makes me feel at home on either side of the Mason-Dixon Line. Of course, the Yankees drove me down south and the Southerners tried to give me back. No wonder I came to LA.

SECTIONAL HEALING

A rhythm section is a complex entity. I try not to use big words such as "complex" and "entity", as they tend to confuse musicians. However, I took this opportunity to cram both words into one sentence and it made me feel more smarter. A rhythm section is a bassist and a drummer rolled into one, sometimes referred to as a "bummer." Ain't that the truth! When a section works, it's beautiful. If it's broken, fix it. Cure it. Heal it.

A section is 2 players, 2 personalities and 2 interpretations of the groove. A good rhythm section understands each others approach to the song. They trust each other to fill in the gaps and/or leave the necessary spaces to make the song work. Locking in to a groove can be a lot more difficult than it appears.

The drummer should start simple with 2 and 4 on the kick and snare. The bassist should stick with the traditional root/5th pattern. This is where the dance begins. More complex rhythms will develop.

Either player will play busier at times. A good section will never get in the way of the other players. Sometimes a rehearsal becomes a tightrope to be walked. Leaning too much to either side can be fatal. The first pass at the song might be too fast. The bass was far too busy on the second pass.

The third attempt starts to make sense and everyone feels the song come together. A lot of young players should follow my 3 rhythm section rules: Abide, ride and subdivide.

-Abide by the basic rule of listening to each other. Adjust your playing to each other until it feels right. You have to know what the other guy is playing in order to make the parts work together.

-When you get the groove right, ride it for a while. Don't change it. Keep it simple but focus on every note. You'll feel it in your bones when you get it. Fight the urge to play something more difficult. A musically challenging part is not necessarily better for the song.

When a solo or bridge is introduced, subdivide by playing 1/8 notes in place of 1/4 notes, or vice versa. This will give the song a little nudge without breaking the groove. This should make for a subtle "change of color", giving the part a different energy and the song a little more substance. This ability to change the color of the song is an art form in itself. It's particularly effective when recording. When done properly, the listener should be able to tell the difference between a verse and a chorus just by listening to the rhythm tracks.

These 3 steps will get both of you up and running as a team. You can fine tune it from there. You will learn to help each other. You can teach each other a lot.

Unless you're working with Young Steve. Steve is a great drummer. In fact, he's a fantastic musician who plays several instruments. He reads and writes music very well. He is a true genius. There is very little that I could teach him about music. He needs none of my advice.
That is why I routinely kick his ass in sports trivia in order to elevate myself. Steve is younger, better looking and more talented than I, so I must mark my territory in typical Alpha Dog fashion. I can't tell him anything about music, but I can intimidate him with physical harm, as he is of slight build and bruises easily. Steve understands this. He endures. He becomes stronger. I am the best thing that has ever happened to him. I tell him so every gig.

BOTTOM LINE:

Much of the SECTIONAL HEALING chapter is aimed at newer players just getting started, but I'm sure there are plenty of seasoned players that could use a reminder. After all, I've been driving a car for 30 years, yet I don't know how well I would do on a DMV road test. Remember all that "hands at 10 and 2" stuff? I surely don't. I would make a fool of myself if I had to go back to my 7th grade English class and diagram a sentence. Maybe this chapter will serve as a quick refresher course to a few players. Is there any chance that Young Steve might learn something from me after all?

DRUM CHART

Boom! Bang! Ok, wait a second. Now, hit the snare. Really fast! Keep going, keep going!! Crash, crash, crash. Stop. Now, really loud with your foot on the big drum. That's it! Twirl a stick and point at the crowd. Stop playing when I stop playing.

Rest.

Repeat.

ONE IS THE LONELIEST NUMBER

Why are they called solo gigs? There are very few solos. If you're playing by yourself, it's not a solo gig. It's loneliness, usually leading directly to depression. However, we shall refer to these gigs as solo gigs for the sake of consistency. I'll go with the flow. After all, I'm easy.

Solo gigs are a great opportunity to play every song you like. You can make thousands of songs fit the solo guitar or piano format if you give it a little thought and creativity. You obviously don't try to sound like the recording, as even the sparse acoustic recordings often have some other instrumentation. Still, it can be fun and challenging.

Playing solo is the opportunity to be inventive, stripping down big production songs to their core and presenting them in an entirely different light. It is also an opening to get stinking drunk without judgment from fellow band mates. You are the center of attention, which means your chances of picking up chicks increase exponentially. (If the performer is a chick, her chance of rejecting a desperate husband hiding his wedding ring is incalculable.) These perks can be distracting, so you should probably focus on the inventive aspect of the performance.

Solo gigs are tougher than they look. I am a terrible solo artist. I am much better suited for a duo or band situation. I prefer to play interactively with another musician. I admire those players that are convincing all by themselves. It truly is an art form.

The pay is often better on a solo gig. The tips can really make a difference. No patron tips 4 times as much for a 4 piece band. A 5 dollar tip for the solo goes right in your pocket. This will help dull the intense pain of isolation as you eat and drink alone in a bar at 2 AM, mirroring the sub-standard existence of that so-called personal life of yours. Soon, you will quit music to become the director of shuffle board on a low level cruise ship so you'll never have to be alone again. Of course, your 17 cats will die of starvation while you're out at sea.

BOTTOM LINE:

Once again, my bitterness rears its ugly head. I'm a terrible solo artist and I'm envious.

THE ACOUSTIC DUO
(SUCKING IN STEREO)

I have spent at least half of my career in acoustic duos. The duo gig is great. It's low maintenance, requiring very little gear and a small PA. It's a low volume gig and I think I've made it clear how appealing that is to me. There is plenty of work, as many small clubs and restaurants that can't accommodate a full band can always make room for a duo.

I use the term acoustic duo because most of my time was spent with two of us playing acoustic guitars and singing. I see this as the easiest way to go. A keyboard takes up too much room, no matter what the keyboardist tells you. 2 guitars can fit in even the smallest of spaces. I try to stick with that format as much as possible.

I made a career of playing happy hours and off nights. Wednesday evenings were always a favorite. We were the only act working, so all our musician friends would come to hear us. We worked 2 gigs every Thursday for almost 4 years. I would drive 60 miles to Upland, Ca. every Thursday to play the happy hour from 5 -8 PM. After throwing guitars into the trunk and white knuckling down the highway, we started playing at 9 PM at a hotel in downtown LA some 40 miles away. I also did a double every Saturday for the better part of ten years by squeezing in an afternoon duo gig before my night time band gigs.

It is easy to book a duo. It's easy to rehearse, record and choose songs. There are only 2 personalities with which to deal. You know right away if it's going to work out. The duo is as much about chemistry as it is music. A duo is not twice as much entertainment as a solo act. It is ten times as much entertainment. The second player adds a different lead voice, harmonies and some guitar solos. It's another onstage persona that will connect to the audience. You know, the cute one, the funny one, etc. (I was never the cute one. Damn those pretty boys! Apparently, I'm not the funny one, either. I guess I should add "bitter" to that list.) If the other guy in your duo is an idiot, you'll be the intellect. If the other guy is the lady killer, then he'll bring a crowd of women and you can have his leftovers. This is a win/win except for the women who wind up dating you.

Of course, a duo is still a musical act and that means there is plenty of potential for things to be awful. An awful 5 piece band can play loud and throw in enough sax solos to make people think they're a cool R&B band. An awful duo does not have that luxury. They must wallow in the muck and mire of bad harmonies and wrong chords. They can't hide behind volume. They can't fill the dance floor with the standard disco beat. They are completely exposed. Of course, they will still get booked every Wednesday and twice every Thursday. Believe me, I know.

You need to approach the duo gig with some real musicality. All too often, 2 members of a 4 piece band think they can automatically become a duo. They think they can simply perform the same songs and play the same parts as they do with their larger band and it will all be fantastic. That's not usually the case. As previously mentioned, you need to approach this with some real musicality, and musicality is often overlooked. A bass and a piano duo playing Sinatra tunes might work fine, but the Justin Timberlake songs could suffer without a little extra attention. This is serious stuff. You need to cover a lot of sonic landscape with 2 players.

I said earlier that rehearsing a duo is "easy." It is easy in the sense that the right players will instinctively and intuitively gravitate to the right tunes. The right guitarist will go for the necessary musical parts, covering the key trumpet solo or prominent piano rhythm in order to make the performance viable. It takes some work. It takes some thought. You have to make it easy.

My duos have been hired for an unbelievable amount of private parties. A couple would hear us in a club. They would ask for my card and call a few days later. They decided to have a backyard party and hire us. The pay was always good, sometimes exceptional. We never worked for less than $250 per man. The same folks would hire us year after year for birthdays, Christmas parties, July 4th and any other reason to have a party. These loyal customers turned this private party thing into a cottage industry. The house party is the best kept secret in rock n roll. It is custom made for a duo.

BOTTOM LINE:

Duos force both players to play the prominent parts of every song. This keeps the integrity of the tune and is a great way to learn the songs properly. The harmonies will be clear as there will be no "gang vocals." The guitar parts will be exposed, not hidden behind a wall of noise. It is the best training imaginable. Do it right and you'll never be out of work.

3 BLIND MICE

If you want to be louder than the duo but less musical than the quartet, the trio is your answer. A common trio is guitar, bass and drums. This configuration is the ultimate in musical freedom and expression as long as you're not the drummer or the bassist.

This trio is a fine opportunity for the guitarist to solo until his wrists swell to twice their original size. On these trio gigs, Solo Boy will play every inversion of every chord he has ever learned, yet, somehow it all winds up sounding like the blues. It is tremendous fun, but only for Solo Boy and his new girlfriend. The future Mrs. Solo Boy is convinced that she has fallen in love with the next musical icon. She has learned all there is to know about the music business in their last 2 lunch dates and is now his manager. It is a match made on the Stairway to Heaven.

There are other trio configurations that are equally as annoying and unfulfilling. Drums, piano and sax is always cause for heavy drinking. As a "DPS" trio, adding a 3 minute ending to a 3 minute song seems to be the prime directive. Sometimes, the pianist sings. He's more of an interpreter than a crooner. In all fairness, he's more of a putz. He warbles for a few moments and then flashes the "dig me smile" that indicates he knows he's fantastic and we're all just lucky to be there. The sax player still has melted cheese stuck to his beard and the drummer hasn't opened his eyes since he parked the car. It's more than music. It's theater.

My personal fave is the TRIO FROM HELL. This is a female vocalist who doesn't play an instrument backed by 2 players who don't sing. It doesn't matter which instruments you put in the hands of these doofs. It's a waste of time, money, space, frets, strings and oxygen. Am I making myself clear? The chick singer usually advertises that she can sing anything from Rosemary Clooney to Celine Dion. This often means she can't sing anything but Rosemary Clooney or Celine Dion. (Author's note: I have nothing but the highest regard for both of these artists. Yet, I don't think anyone could possibly sit in a cocktail lounge all night listening to only that material-with the possible exceptions of Ms. Rosemary Clooney and Ms. Celine Dion.)

BOTTOM LINE:

If you're going to have 3 people on stage, make them all bring something to the table. Try some backing vocals. C'mon, humor an old man!!

THE FANTASTIC FOUR

I love working with a 4 piece band. It seems to be the perfect situation. Duos and trios are fine, but they're not really considered bands. They're considered duos and trios. A 4 piece band is a band, not a quartet. A quartet is a string section that plays stuff from the Viennese Period or some such nonsense. In fact, I think you are required to have a European accent in order to play in a quartet. A 4 piece band is pure rock n roll. It is 4 distinct personalities, sometimes clashing but always creating great music.

The FPB is big enough for any wedding, club or concert but small enough to travel light. One mini van or 2 small cars will transport this outfit across town and across the country. 2 hotel rooms will suffice. One all- you- can- eat buffet will do nicely.

The FPB will undoubtedly be a drummer, a bassist and a guitarist. The fourth member should be a second guitarist or keyboardist. If you have trouble finding that guy, call my friend Jeff. He plays both guitar and keys and sings very well. Don't call him right now because he usually sleeps late. Friday afternoons are no good because he has lunch with his wife. Maybe give him a ring on Wednesday afternoon, sometime between 2 and 3:30…no, that won't work. You might need to find someone else after all.

Upon finding that fourth guy that isn't Jeff, you're all set. Now, it's understood that at least 3 of you have to sing. Otherwise, you won't be able to do the Beatle harmonies. If you are the new guy and you can't do the Beatle harmonies, you shouldn't be in the band. You're fired! Get out! You disgust me! Out! Now! Do as I say!

No pizza for you!

BOTTOM LINE:

Looks like you're a trio again.

4 + 1=5 MOST OF THE TIME

You have a great 4 piece rock band. You work steadily in the clubs, but you want to make a little more money. The clearest path to better money is the wedding band. The 4 + 1 is the most popular configuration for wedding bands. The clearest and easiest way to get wedding gigs is to add a girl singer to your great 4 piece rock band.

I'm going to read your mind right now. You're thinking, "Bill makes adding a girl singer to my already successful act sound simple. He's setting me up for a fall. He's now going to spend the next 3 paragraphs telling me how difficult this will be."

That was, indeed, my initial intent. After thinking about it for a moment, I came to the conclusion that adding a singer really doesn't have to be difficult at all. I've done it several times with tremendous results. I can give you a blueprint to follow. If taken seriously, it can help you get the better paying gigs without wasting any time or effort.

We are starting with the premise that you have a solid, working band. You sound good and tight, you have enough material to play 4 sets and you have the equipment you need. You require the singer to bring in 16 songs needed for the typical wedding. Let's say she brings in 4 very current up-tempo tunes, 4 ballads, 4 standards and 4 Motown tunes. The band probably knows several of the Motown tunes and is familiar with a few of the standards, so these 16 songs shouldn't take too long to learn. If the girl is a working singer, she probably has a book with charts. That will make the process a lot easier.

Adding these types of songs will give you the song list you need for any wedding. Now, add 25 appropriate songs from your club act. Obviously, depressing and profane lyrics have no place at a wedding. Some might think it to be cool, but Aunt Rose isn't gonna dig it. Trust me, there's an Aunt Rose at every wedding. It's the law. Play your strongest material. Don't ever be afraid to rock at a wedding. After all, it's often a great family party. People want to dance and celebrate.

They won't need much encouragement. They just need the band to lead them in the right direction.

Adding the girl singer adds a whole new dimension to the band. She will immediately be the focal point. Use this to your advantage. Showcase her voice by letting her sing exactly what she wants in her key. Use her falsetto for the upper harmonies on your rock songs. Give her a tambourine. She certainly doesn't have to learn all 40 of your club tunes, but it would be a nice touch to see her more involved with the band. She is a member now, not a guest singer. If she is able to do some of the announcing or MC work, so much the better.

The wedding vibe is different than the club vibe. The guys need black suits, black ties and maybe tuxes. We rarely worry about the girl. She knows what to wear. She's a girl, for goodness sake. The band plays the appropriate songs at a reasonable volume. The music is coordinated with the serving of food. A club set is 45 minutes. A wedding set is determined by when the prime rib is ready. Somebody in the band has to be the Master of Ceremonies. "Thank you, ladies and gentlemen. I'd like to ask you all to return to your seats as dinner is now being served. We are The Velvets and we'll be back in a few. Enjoy!" These announcements are absolutely crucial to the flow and direction of the party. You tell the audience when it's time to eat, time to clear the floor for the Father and Daughter dance and when the cake is being cut. Get it down pat and you'll be golden. Of course, you will only call yourselves The Velvets on wedding dates. The band can still call themselves The Flying Rat Boys on the club circuit.

Let's recap. You already have a cool rock band. You add a girl singer in order to get wedding gigs for good money. She brings her own repertoire with charts. The band learns 16 songs, most of them familiar. The chick learns a handful of harmonies on your rock songs and does some of the announcements. You guys supply the PA. This whole situation will be fantastic. No one puts in too much work. The gigs are well organized. The money is good and people love you. It's all good.

BOTTOM LINE:

Now, pray that chick doesn't get PMS on a gig. If she does, it's not a 4+1. It's a 4 against 1 and the four of you will lose that fight. During "that time", she is Godzilla and you are 4 helpless Japanese citizens trying to escape through the back alleys of Tokyo. This is no casual analogy on my part. The red eyed Godzilla breathes fire and destroys everything in its path.

Admit it, ladies. That's you once a month.

SOUL CRUSHERS

Most gigs are rewarding in one way or another. We've covered those. There are a few gigs that simply fall through the cracks, offering diminishing returns and eventually having no redeeming value. These gigs are called "soul crushers".

I have tried to avoid this topic. I have failed. It's unavoidable. Soul crushers find their way into your life. They sneak up on you. It's usually your fault. You gave your card to someone and said, "Hey, if you ever need a drummer call me." The next week, they called you for a Thursday night gig. It was a 75 mile drive and it only paid 80 bucks, but you figured "What the Hell, I'm not doing anything else." That gig has turned into 3 weekends per month.

You have quickly come to hate this gig. You never really wanted it, but you did it anyway. Then, the rest of the band asked you if you were having fun. You said all the right things. "Dude, you guys are great! Am I having fun? Are you kidding me? I'm having the time of my life!" You thought you were being professional. These words came back to bite you in the ass.

Let's take a moment to discuss this "bite you in the ass" phrase. When you accidentally volunteer to help your neighbor clean out his garage or pick up your in –laws from the airport, that's bitten in the ass. But when you find yourself in a soul crusher, it takes bitten to a whole new level. This is not the garage or the airport. This is that baby alligator that you flushed down the toilet. It has lived in the sewer for years, getting bigger and stronger and angrier everyday until it retraces it's amphibious steps and propels itself up out of the porcelain, locking it's jaws around your glutes at your most vulnerable and exposed time and drags you back down through the elbow pipe and into the abyss in a death spiral, leaving only your sandals and your hat on the bathroom floor. The MCSI (Musical Crime Scene Investigators) were called. They took one look and nodded to each other. "Soul crusher. Shame. He was a good drummer. A damn good drummer."

As of the time of this writing, I am trying desperately to get out of a soul crusher. I have been doing this gig for almost 4 years, totaling over 120 dates. It's a theme park gig and I was there when the job started. I hated it the first day. I thought it would get easier because the band was great. As the gig went on, we involved more players, all of whom were fantastic musicians and great people. Still, I hated the gig.

I did my best to do a good job. When I felt as if I was burning out, I asked the musical director for some time off. He gave me all the time I needed. I came back refreshed a month later and immediately hated the gig again. I ran the numbers. The money was OK. The gig was steady and close to home. The band was great and the friendships were even better. What was the problem?

The friggin hat! That was my answer when the MD asked why I was quitting for the third time in 4 years. I could not stand to wear the stupid little hat with the stupid little uniform. I was embarrassed to be seen in it. Every once in a while, a friend would come to the theme park and recognize me. I would cringe. It killed me everyday. It took a little piece of me each gig. It crushed my soul on a daily basis.

Why did I continue to do this gig? Excellent question! I stayed to pay the rent. I stayed because I didn't want to become one of those whiny musicians who complained all the time. I wanted to get out of my comfort zone. I wanted to push myself and show some discipline. I hoped a gig of this nature would stop me from taking myself too seriously and take a more relaxed approach to music. I thought a little departure from my other gigs would give me some perspective. I thought it would make me humble.

I wasn't necessarily wrong about any of these. This gig did allow me to make some much needed money and develop some great relationships. It did challenge me and push me out of my comfort zone.

It also crushed my soul.

This day is the moment of truth for me. I have read my own words in this book and I should take my own advice. I did my best for as long as possible. I tried not to let the band suffer because of my unhappiness. I never showed up unprepared and never slacked off. I took time off when I needed it. I was always up front and honest with the boss. Now, it's time to leave this gig that is sapping so much of my energy. It's time to put this behind me. Should I fake my own death? The idea of a new identity with no connection to the theme park gig is enticing. Enticing, yes. Practical, no. Changing my name would mean losing all my frequent flyer miles. I'll just take the high road. I will resign today. I will no longer do the soul crusher.

BOTTOM LINE:

Soul crushers can build character and make you appreciate other gigs. Keep that in mind because you'll have to do a few soul crushers in your career.

DIFFICULT CROSSWORD PUZZLE
(Particularly for bassists)

ACROSS

    1. musician
    2. favorite eating place of musician

DOWN

    1. world's greatest food
    2. musician

NOTE: someone said one of these answers is misspelled. It's probably the same clown who thought there was an "X" in zylophone! Yeesh!! Meanwhile, there are no numbered squares, the clues have been answered and the puzzle was designed in magic marker. Still, by all means, congratulate yourself on having such a critical eye as to catch the typo!

GIGS IN SPACE

Years ago, my big time manager asked me how he thought our band could make a splash in the industry. I suggested we be the first band to play on the space shuttle. At the time, the idea seemed preposterous. Now, it seems as though that concept is right around he corner.

I have spent a good deal of this book writing about the past. It's time we look to the future. The next generation blue collar musician might not be a rock star, but he might be a pioneer. As BCMs, we innately possess the pioneer spirit of our forefathers. We will push the envelope and take the 17 year trip to circumnavigate Mercury and return to Earth. This gig will be booked and an agent will take his cut. Can you imagine? A 15% commission of the gig funded by the space program? That agent will calmly walk into the NASA office and collect his check for $2,436,365,678.36. Then, he'll ask to have his have his parking validated.

The interplanetary gig will be intense. It's a commitment. An extensive song list will be needed. You will have to download the newest songs on a daily basis. Of course, by the time the signal reaches you in outer space, these songs will be oldies on Earth. If this concept confuses you, google Einstein and give it a once over.

A band performing on an interplanetary cruise will happen, as soon as NASA figures out how to keep the shrimp fresh at the buffet. It will be a grueling gig for sure. It will be hard to keep the show exciting. "Thank you, I'm Bobby Neptune and I'll be here for the next 545 Thursdays. Enjoy the Venus veal!" You'll have the same audience every night, as no one can leave. That means one thing. You will get laid.

Think it through. What kind of girl gets on a rocket ship for 17 years? A desperate one. That's a plus for you. The married women will be divorced soon enough. The prepubescent girls will come of age on this flight. The mature MILFS will most likely die before you dock. This is all in your favor.

This gig will lead to other gigs. These cruises will become commonplace and turn the planets and their moons into vacation destinations. This will bring clubs and casinos to these places, giving the astro-musicians a lot of work. Acts such as The Final Frontier Band, The No One Can Hear You Scream Project and Danger, Will Robinson will headline the coolest clubs on the scene. This will be good for you. It will cut the flight time in half. You'll only have to go one way. Then, you can dump one milf and pick up another for the ride home. Rock on!

REALLY GOOD MUSIC TRIVIA

I love music trivia. Either you know the answers or you learn something. It's always fun. It never has to be a formal game with dice or scorecards. You can just sit around with a few friends and have a good time.

I will list a few questions here. These are not the obvious softball no brainers from TV GUIDE. These are tough. Of course, some of my hardcore older musician friends will scoff at many of these, but for the average Joe, I think these will be a challenge. Let's see how you do.

1. Name the first 2 drummers from the Average White Band.
2. What TV theme was performed by Alabama 3?
3. Who wrote TAKE 5?
4. Name Nirvana's bassist.
5. Who recorded WALKING ON SUNSHINE?
6. Joss Stone and Melissa Etheridge performed what 2 songs at the 2005 Grammys? (Joss did the first one by herself and Etheridge joined her for second song)
7. What song featured the first recorded synthesizer?
8. Martin Scorsese directed movies featuring 2 iconic bands. Name the movies and the bands.
9. What is Usher's real name?
10. What record company had both The Shins and Soundgarden on their roster?
11. What is the name of the unique instrument featured in Good Vibrations? (hint: a lot of people get this one wrong)
12. Flea endorses which brand of bass?
13. Who is the only drummer to ever record on every track of a STEELY DAN record?
14. Name all 3 members of La Belle.
15. What movie featured the first Cobra Starship hit?
16. Tim Rice-Oxley, Tom Chaplin and Richard Hughes are all members of what band?
17. What is the real name of L.A. Reid's producing partner?

18. Mariah Carey had a hit with what Badfinger song?

19. Who played Doyle in Slingblade?

20. What was the name of Elvis Presley's back up singers?

REALLY GOOD TRIVIA ANSWERS

1. Robbie MacIntosh, Steve Ferrone
2. The Sopranos
3. Paul Desmond
4. Krist Novoselic
5. Katrina and the Waves
6. Cry, Baby/Another Piece of My Heart
7. Runaway by Del Shannon
8. The Rolling Stones, Shine A Light. The Band, The Last Waltz
9. Usher Raymond IV
10. Sub Pop Records
11. The tannerin, although many think it is a theramin. According to Wikipedia: Contrary to popular belief, the theremin was not used on the 1966 recording of "Good Vibrations" by The Beach Boys, which featured Paul Tanner's "box", later called the electro-theremin. However, for concert appearances, an oscillator slide-controller was designed and built for Wilson by Robert Moog. Wilson helped to popularize the instrument when he recorded Paul Tanner playing his electro-theremin -- for the first time in recorded music history -- on the song "I Just Wasn't Made For These Times." The song appeared on The Beach Boys' 1966 album Pet Sounds, considered one of the most influential albums in popular music history.
12. Modulus
13. Keith Carlock
14. Patti La Belle, Nona Hendrix, Sara Dash
15. Snakes On A Plane
16. Keane
17. Kenneth Edmonds
18. Without You
19. Dwight Yoakum
20. The Jordanaires

PLACING SONGS IN TV AND FILM

Many musicians find a lot of success placing their songs in TV shows and movies. That is, many writers find success. When a song generates money, the writer is the person who will collect the royalties. Writing a good song is always a tough assignment. We always try to write a "good" song. Once in a while, we are successful. Sometimes, the success is because of hard work, trial and error, writing and rewriting. Other times it's an accident. There are those rarest of moments when the entire song just comes to you in full arrangement and lyrics. Some might call that Divine Intervention. The musical gods decided to give you a little nudge in writing that elusive good song.

What is good?

Good question. Is there a good answer? Well, there certainly isn't a short one. Defining what is "good" in music is never easy. You hate that annoying song you keep hearing on the radio, but believe me, you wish you had written it. It's making money every single time you hate it.

It doesn't have to be a hit song. It could be a jingle for a local bank or restaurant. Is it effective? If it is, then it's good. It was designed to be memorable and satisfy the need of the client, namely to have their jingle stick in your head.

You write a song and play it on stage at a local gig. People like it. They are hearing it for the first time, but by the second chorus, they're singing along with you. That's a good song. You connected with the audience. If you write a song for your 2 year old daughter to help sing her to sleep, you'll know immediately if it's a good song. You won't need a royalty check to validate it.

I have already stated that this book is not aimed at getting a record deal. However, you can make money from your recorded music by getting your material placed in movies or television shows. It can be quite a challenge, but you knew the job was dangerous when you took it. Let me give you a quick overview of song placement.

The people responsible for putting the music in TV shows are called music supervisors. Their primary job is choosing the appropriate song for the scene. They will look at the script or the film and decide they need a high energy, guitar driven song for the high speed chase scene, a soft jazz instrumental for the love scene and so on. If they have some of your music available to them, they might choose one of your songs for the show.

If you can get your music directly to the music supervisor, you are ahead of the game. Sometimes, that can be difficult. Often, the "supe" uses a publisher or a music library to get the needed material. They call their contact and ask for exactly what they require. The requests might look something like this:

1. Soft ballad, 66 beats per minute, female vocal, sax solo, lyrics re: heartbreak

2. Hard rock, 133 bpm, screaming male vocals, big harmonies on chorus

If you can develop a relationship with a supervisor, publisher or music library, you have a shot at placing songs on film and TV. I can tell you from personal experience that listening to your song on a nationally televised show is quite a thrill. Seeing your name in the screen credits of a motion picture is pretty cool as well. I hate to toot my own horn here, but if my name looks familiar to you, it's probably because you've seen it in the closing credits for the 1989 riveting masterpiece, PHANTOM OF THE MALL, starring Morgan Fairchild and Paulie Shore. I have no doubt many of you will rent the movie just to see if I'm telling the truth. That's fine by me. I think POTM is an important film and a cinematic treasure that should be appreciated by the masses. Honestly, I rented it on VHS the week it came out. I fast forwarded to the ending credits until I saw my name.

The next year, I moved to LA. I hooked up with a working band. I soon co-wrote and recorded songs with Dave, the lead singer. Song placements were not a priority for either of us at that time. I had my one claim to fame in that area and we spent most of our time and energy playing live, chasing the big record deal.

A few years later, Dave started attending conferences and "demo derbies" where, for a fee, your music could be reviewed and critiqued by industry professionals. One day, he got a call saying 15 seconds of one of his songs would be placed on a daytime soap opera. Slowly but surely, over the next few months, several of Dave's songs were used on TV. Then, a few of our co-writes were being placed. Eventually, a publisher called Dave and said, "Who is that man Bill with the glorious voice doing your background vocals? I simply must have more material with that man singing. He's angelic. He's otherworldly. He's a vocal phenomenon!" That's my version, anyway.

Dave and I started writing songs with me singing lead. It led to a lot of placements for both of us. He did the "whiskey and cigarettes" voice and I did the "smooth R&B" voice. These descriptions became a bit of a joke for us, as we let go of our egos and just went with the flow. We recorded mostly in Dave's garage. It became evident which one of us would be better suited to sing the requested tune. We stockpiled songs on our own and became proficient at writing songs on short notice to fill the needs of the supes. A Monday morning call for a 50's sounding doo wop song in ¾ often resulted in an all day writing and recording session, ending in a midnight mix and a polite thank you to some very understanding neighbors.

As our business grew, we brought more people into the circle. In the early days, we wrote, sang, played all the instruments, programmed drums and mixed. Once again letting go of our egos, we began working with Per, a gifted musician/producer who had the knack for making every song sound better. It's been about 15 years and 700 song placements. The 3 of us still work together today. This is probably a good time to thank Dave for getting this ball rolling and Per for keeping it going in the right direction.

OK, that's as mushy as I get. Back to the business at hand. You've written and recorded the song. You've gotten it to a publisher who has passed it on to the music supervisor of the hit daytime soap opera, THE WRINKLED YEARS. TWY, as we call it in the biz, needs your song titled I HOPE THESE AREN'T SHARK INFESTED WATERS 'CAUSE I STILL LOVE YOU. This song is perfect because the scene is…can you guess where this is going? Your song is placed in the show and a week later, millions of viewers get to hear it on TV. Hold on to that feeling of satisfaction and excitement as long as you can. Your payment in the form of a check from ASCAP, BMI or SEASAC might very well take 9 months to get to you. You see, the year is broken into quarters and the pay is usually 3 quarters, or 9 months from the air date. I always thought it was rather poetic that the gestation period is the same for babies and royalty payments. The song is aired and then the writer waits nervously as the due date for the check approaches. Sure, you could make a phone call and find out the exact amount that you will receive, but that's tantamount to a sonogram. I'd rather be surprised. Of course, if the check is a few days late, resist the temptation to give the mailbox a C-section. It doesn't help.

BOTTOM LINE:

TARA'S THEME from Gone with the Wind and BOHEMIAN RHAPSODY by Queen are great songs. So are HAPPY BIRTHDAY and CHOPSTICKS. A good song is not based on musical complexity. Take any approach you like. There's no formula for songwriting. You'll know a good song when you write it. Hopefully, it can make you some money.

4 OUT OF 5 DENTISTS CHOOSE DENTISTRY OVER KARAOKE

If you enjoy an evening of drinking with some friends in a Karaoke bar, you are a fun loving person who goes for the gusto in life. If you are a wanna be singer going to a karaoke bar in an attempt to further your career, all I can say is… wow!

The karaoke stage is for drunken people who can't sing. That's what makes it funny. It's not for singers who are trying to impress someone. It's not an audition. It's not a real gig. No one should get laid singing Karaoke.

I'm not knocking the karaoke business. I'm knocking the people that take themselves too seriously when they sing at these places. It should be a loose atmosphere where the average person can lose his inhibitions, jump up on stage and sing, bark or whatever to an audience that will support you no matter what. If you've ever been in attendance, you'll know that I'm serious about the "no matter what" part.

The average guy or girl takes the stage with a shaky voice and very little experience, usually needing the lyrics and some bourbon to get through the tune. It takes some courage to put one's self out there like that. Now, how is that novice going to feel when a seasoned singer gets up right before? I would guess the answer is intimidated. There is no place for intimidation in a karaoke bar!! If there were, the place would go out of business.

These performances shouldn't turn into a talent contest because it's not a level playing field. 3 salesmen come in and talk their boss into singing Hit Me Baby, One More Time. The boss should not be competing with the "Little Miss Look At Me" with the tight skirt and 8 years of vocal lessons. It's unfair. This is why there are weight classes in boxing. It's unfair to have a heavyweight fight a lightweight, unless it's me and Steve, the younger and better looking drummer. Man, I would stomp him out!

Salesmen and dock workers should go to Karaoke bars and have the time of their lives after a hard day's work. They don't go to hear the best singer in town. They go to be goofy for a few hours. Nobody cares how well you sing. In fact, we particularly don't care. We care about a lot of things, but the talent level at the Karaoke bar is not one of them. If you are a singer, go to an open mic or jam night and hone your craft. We'll all be very supportive of you in that environment. You'll need our support. You probably suck.

BOTTOM LINE

Does Karaoke need a bottom line? Does this require any more explanation? Maybe so. Here is a likely scenario.

5 dentists go to a Bruce Springsteen concert. They watch and listen as 19,000 people sing the words to every one of Bruce's songs. These dentists each have a moment in which the following thoughts are running through their heads. "Man, I would give up my practice in a minute if I thought I could be on stage with Bruce. Maybe I chose the wrong career path. I'm confused. I'm at odds with myself. Should I follow my childhood dream of being a backup singer? After all, I was pretty good in junior high."

These moments of self doubt happen all the time. There is a remedy for this feeling of uncertainty. These 5 guys should go directly to a karaoke bar after the Springsteen concert. They should each get on stage and sing. 4 out of 5 will realize that dentistry is the right choice.

Of course, Dentist # 5 will abandon his practice in order to pursue his new career as back up singer/financier of Little Miss Look At Me in the tight skirt. Stupid bastard. He should realize nobody gets laid at karaoke.

I AM NOT NOW NOR WILL I EVER BE READY FOR MY CLOSE UP

I needed some photos taken of me for this book. I don't really know why. A book should be about my words, not my appearance. Being both stupid and ugly, it became clear that I would lose on either front, so I had some pictures taken.

I truly hate having my picture taken. I have always been very comfortable in front of a microphone but not so in front of a camera. I suddenly become self conscious and reticent. I don't know how to pose. I can never relax my eyebrows. I always look angry in photos. That's because there is a camera in my face and I hate cameras. I feel like I'm in the cross hairs of a sniper's rifle.

As you can understand, this can be a problem when a photo shoot is required. My tolerance runs thin during the 12 seconds it takes for my DMV photo. I say things like "Do I have to stand on the yellow line? Just snap the thing and get it over with!" How will I ever get through a photo session? Session. The word itself conjures up therapy and a couch, both of which I might need by the end of the day.

I called my good friend, Kevin. He's an interesting guy. He's a musician, a songwriter and a photographer. He agreed to step into the lion's den and take my picture. He's a great photographer. I'm a terrible subject. This means if we get a good shot, it's all because of him. If we don't, it's all because of me. I can do no right. I am suddenly the Charlie Brown of the shutterbug community. Good grief!

I brought several shirts. Kevin examined each of them with a critical eye, saying "Yeah, yeah, this could work. These are fantastic." He immediately threw my stuff aside and made me wear one of his shirts. So much for fantastic. I wasn't insulted, as my sense of style runs from unflattering to doofus. My fashion sense tells me that a New York Giants "home" jersey is formal wear and the "away" jersey is cocktail casual. It's not easy being me.

We started with some outdoor shots in order to utilize the natural light. I have no idea why natural light is preferred, but I went with the flow. I walked, sat, leaned, turned and walked some more on command. My responses would be the envy of everyone at the American Kennel Club. Kevin was terrific. It was difficult for me to be there in the first place. I feared a friend shooting the photos might heighten my embarrassment, but all went well. Kevin was able to get me to express my full range of emotions. Direction such as "Say cheese" and "Give me bewildered" were immediately replaced by "Think of pizza with extra sauce" and "Let's bring it down a little....the pizza is cold." I couldn't help but laugh because it worked. I was relaxed despite the bazooka with a lens that was pointed at me.

Later, we took more shots at his home studio. I tried on a few shirts in his living room. The neighbors must have thought, "Poor Kevin. Business must be tough. That's the shabbiest male model I've ever seen!" Good grief!

In 4 hours, Kevin had taken 700 pictures of me. Wouldn't it have been easier to just photo shop some gray hair on Brad Pitt and call it a day? Brad has always been big on charity. Would anyone care? After all, it's a book. It's about my words, not my appearance. I soon realized that I would have to bite the bullet and use my own photo. I apologize.

Redhead Talent Management & Photography
Kevin Still
www.redheadphotography.ifp3.com

CARNEGIE HALL

As a native New Yorker, I have attended several shows at Carnegie Hall. I performed at a little bar just down the street from Carnegie. I recorded across the street from the famous venue. I used to stare out the window while eating at the Carnegie Deli, all the while dreaming of what it might be like to play in the famous setting. For much of my life, I was close, but no cigar. That all changed on Wednesday, October 10, 2007. On that day I had the pleasure of performing at Carnegie Hall, the greatest stage in the world. It was the most thrilling gig of my life.

Peter and Gordon, along with 17 other acts, had been invited to perform at a tribute to the music of Elton John and Bernie Taupin. Each act did one Elton John song. A house band backed up many of the other acts. In our case, Peter and Gordon elected to bring our own band for this very special performance. I am eternally grateful that they did.

We found out on Wednesday, October 3rd that we would be playing the following Wednesday. It could have been a frantic week of rearranging plans, booking flights and taking care of the incredible minutia involved in getting 6 musicians and a manager across the country. Much to our credit, it wasn't frantic at all. In fact, it was all wrapped up in 24 hours. Every member of our organization was well aware of the prestige of Carnegie Hall. Everyone wanted to do it and we made it happen in record time.

Carnegie Hall makes you nervous, no matter how long you've been performing. It was so awe-inspiring just to do the sound check. I looked up into the balconies and remembered sitting up there as a kid. In a few hours, people would line up, buy tickets, take their seats and wait for us to come out onstage and play. It seemed surreal.

Showtime arrived. We watched a good deal of the show on monitors in the dressing room upstairs. From time to time, I ran down to the wings and saw what I could of the other acts onstage. Finally, our moment came. The backstage announcer began our introduction. "This next act came to America in the 60's as part of the British Invasion." People started to applaud before she finished her sentence. The four band members walked out first and took our places. "Ladies and gentlemen, please welcome Peter and Gordon." The place erupted. We played our version of Elton and Bernie's masterpiece, I WANT LOVE, from Elton's 2001 release, SONGS FROM THE WEST COAST, for the closing of the show. It sounded great. It felt great. We ended our one and only song, bowed and walked off the greatest stage in the world to thunderous applause.

I know it was a fantastic experience for everyone involved. I couldn't help thinking I had a little more fun than anyone else. I had walked passed this building a thousand times, feeling so close and yet so far from the stage on the other side of the wall. Close, but no cigar.

We all know the old joke, "How do you get to Carnegie Hall?" As of October 10th, 2007, my punch line has changed.

BOTTOM LINE:

I would sincerely like to thank Mr. Peter Asher and Mr. Gordon Waller for giving me the greatest gift of my musical career.

CLOSING TIME

Well, I guess it's about time I wrapped this thing up. I'm tired of writing and I'm sure you're tired of reading this out loud to all your friends in order to be popular. Ending this book is harder than you might think. It's not a story in which the charming prince saves the day or the secret agent cuts the red wire in order to disarm the ticking bomb. It's an ongoing saga. It can be frustrating, kooky, frustrating, rewarding, inspiring and sometimes frustrating. It's never boring. It's the life of a musician.

My intention was to educate and entertain you with a few cartoons and several real life experiences. I ranted and raved. I laughed at myself and others. I accidentally bared my soul a few times. I say accidentally because I never planned on that. It just happened. Admittedly, the writing of this book has been incredibly therapeutic for me. I'd like to think I opened a few eyes and got a few chuckles. I have no doubt that I rubbed a few people the wrong way, as my liberal use of the words "idiot" and "moron" is bound to get at least a handful of poison pen responses. Hey, I can take it. After all, what's good for the goose is good for the old, fat author.

At the time of this writing, I have done over 4200 gigs. By the time you read it, I will probably (hopefully) have done several more. Several more gigs will result in a little more money, a lot more stories and a ton of great music. Maybe there's a sequel to be written. Who knows?

I guess that depends on you. You already have the book. I would like to hear your opinions and critiques. I expect you to be as honest with me as I have been with you. Feel free to contact me at billcinque.com. Maybe I'll write a sequel or maybe I'll just ride off into the sunset. I guess we'll all find out together. I was never a fan of long goodbyes, so allow me to say thanks for reading. I hope we get to do this again soon.

Meanwhile, I'll see you on the path!

Peace and love,

Bill Cinque

NON-ALPHABETIZED
SPECIAL THANKS

(It's more fun this way! Think of how excited you'll be when you finally locate your name.)

Sam Ash Music

Guitar Center

Taxi (the band)

Jubilee Music

Viking Horn Studios

P.J. Flanders

Matt "Flea" Cinque

Ian Mitchell's Bay City Rollers

The Copy Cats

David Goldman

Margaret Dillon

Joe Testa

Harry McCarthy

Chad and Jeremy

Curb Records

Nathaniel Kunkel

Billy J. and Roni Kramer

Westwood Music

Scotty Millan

John Branca

Taxi (the company)

Eric's Guitar Repair

Scrooge Productions

Kathleen Capper

Keith Putney

Connie Lindell

The Buffalo Inn

Peter Noone

Dennis Miller

The New York Giants

Terry Sylvester

Denny Laine

Hunter and Miles Millan

ASCAP

Heavy Hitters Music

West LA Music

Ann Henningsen

Billy Lamar

Beth Cinque

Lindsay Pietroluongo

The Cryers

Stellar

Andy Pietroluongo

Forest Clinton

Morgan Pearson

Kathy Holland

Chip Hawkes

J.D. Lewis

Niclas Tornell

Emelie Tornell

Tina Tornell

Isabel Tornell

Rick Lynch

Lincoln Smith

Howie Preiser

Bill Aucoin

Kay Grenier

Robert Pratt

Mike Glendinning

Sherwin Bash

Peter Thea

Courtney C. Patty

Mandy Sparks

Lacey Perry

Sound Street Studios

Nola Recording Studios

Barbara Jordan

Naked To The World

Erica Nicole

Elizabeth Farrellee

Carole King

James Taylor

All of New York City, most of Los Angeles and some of Fairhope, Alabama

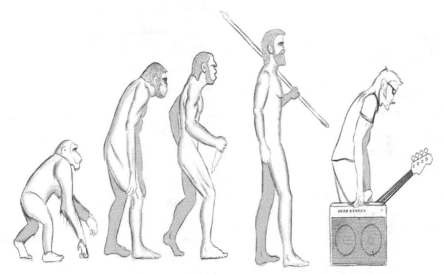

YOU SAY YOU WANT AN EVOLUTION??

cave painting by Matt Cinque
copyright 60,000 years B.C.

Musicians Who Have Shared the Stage and Studio With Me

steve aho
karmine alers
yassmin alers
christopher allis
nick amaroso
andi
jorgen alofs
kirk arthur
chris asberry
peter asher
reggie ashley
frank attanasio
justin avery
steve avitabile
scotty avitabile
greg babcock
mike bacich
john baer
eric baines
john balbuena
damon banks
jamie bannon
bruce becker
chris berardo
marc berardo
george bernardo
dave beyer
fuzzy blagmon
ron blake
dave blasucci
margot boecker
tom bolton
steve bonino
frankie brenna
jono brown
peter buck
cornelius bumpus
guster buster
john button
andy cahan
dave call
colin cameron
joe campbell
darnell cantrell
dave casanova
laurie casanova
dee castro
christina chang
bill cheney
chris cichorek
mark chipello
steve cinque
jeanette clinger
jeremy clyde
fernando cofrese
bobby costantino
ricky costantino
angel curtin
steve curto
jimmy cutrone
thomas dawson
dean delorenzo
dave derge
liberty devitto
hollye dexter
tom diekmeier
bob diekmeier
maureen dougherty
alex drizos

ed eblin
joachim eckberg
skip edwards
roger ehrnman
george eisaman
herman eng
kirk evans
jeff falcone
steve fazio
guy febbraio
martin fera
gary ferguson
lee Ferrell
tom fillman
mike fink
kevin fisher
kelly fitzgerald
walter fowler
eric fraley
dayna franklin
tom friedlander
craig fundyga
bob giammarco
amber gill
tim gill
kiko gonzalez
rory gordon
mike green
michele greene
michael greenfield
jimmy greenspoon
mark gregg
melinda grey
john greyhouse
myron grombacher
david gross
nick gruter

ana guigui
billy haarbauer
kristian habenicht
john hamilton
jason harnell
cooper harris
danny harris
marc harris
barry harrison
bob hawkins
jason hawks
rob hayes
sara haze
john henderson
felice hernandez
mike hines
matt hoecking
frank hoffmeyer
carter holt
chris houchin
alex howland
darren hubacher
steve hunter
joe iaqunito
ruben izquierdo
tilford jackson
david james
bobby jarzombek
erik johnson
matt johnson
tony jones
kylae jordan
jeff joscak
scott kay
jimmy keegan
joe kelly
dwight kennedy

leslie king

per kjeller

tim kobza

peter koehler

billy j. Kramer

andre lafosse

denny laine

teri lamar

scot lang

mike langland

matt laug

wan lee

chelsea lena

pat leon

len leonard

randy levinson

rosie limeres

hank linderman

buc lockwood

jason lomheim

mois lucas

fran lucci

bob luna

john mahon

brian mahoney

bob malone

fred mandell

tony mandracchia

christia mantzke

lisa marinacci

tommy marotta

danny marrone

gerry marsden

andrew martinez

kerry marx

mike mason

ben mauro

early mccallster

christie mccarthy

harry mccarthy

donna mcdaniel

kim mcclain

will mcj

tif mcmillin

don medina

jeff miley

greg miller

mike miller

steve millington

ian mitchell

matt Mitchell

beainy minas

joey molland

joe monroe

shanna morrison

carmen mosier

richard nash

noah needleman

ty nelson

dan nolton

peter noone

steve norde

gary novak

chris o'connell

devon o'day

rich o'neill

david page

cary park

gil parris

yvonne perea

tony pia

john pickel

gary ponder

brian pothier

chaska potter
tom power
ariel powers
chad quist
jackie rae
chris ralles
hal ratliff
eric redd
kathy reese
jerry rennino
iris revson
jimmy riccitelli
rudy richman
jimmy riviera
adam roach
walter roberti
darren ross
jeff alan ross
bill rotella
fino roverato
karl roy
deena russo
patti russo
evyn ryskas
raul sanchez
steve schalchlin
eve selis
daryl silberman
chot simmons
daryl simmons
dave smith
jason smith
philip lincoln smith
smidi smith
sterling smith
kerry song
frank sorci

wes spooner
tiffany splettstoeszer
jeff stillman
chuck st. troy
joey stann
richie steele
eric steigen
peter stirpe
tom stone
jimmy street
chad stuart
sandra grace susino
terry sylvester
steve talbot
todd tatum
mona tavakoli
mike thanasoulis
artie thanasoulis
john thomas
pat thomi
peter tornell
traysee
steve trovato
marc twang
dorothy valentine
joe vetter
kyle vincent
matt waldrum
joe walker
gordon waller
jon walmsley
john walsh
kurt walther
dave wasserman
bruce watson
phil wayne
jimmy welch

lorrie wesoly
brooke wilkes
bobby williams
mark williams
steve wilson
dave woeckener
chad wright
ramon yslas

Also

lionel barton
beth boltuch
ed bydalek
jamie chez
chad clark
paul cooper
kathleen crone
darice
alex davis
fernando diez
bobby dragonetti
david eng
tom farrell
greg fiellen
david goldman
ricardo griego
carmen grillo
brian hardin
john heinzinger
glen herniter
peter knight
joshua lee
debbie lytton-lloyd
rob man
mike mcevoy
john meadows
jonathan mitchell
carol moore

gene moore
dave osti
jennifer persignault
joe piket
airel power
jay prince
dean rubicek
ido sasson
mike sauer
rocky sharer
stuart stahr
john stevens
roman taylor

GORDON WALLER
June 4, 1945-July 17, 2009

CPSIA information can be obtained
at www.ICGtesting.com
Printed in the USA
FSHW011620150720
71607FS

9 781440 115677